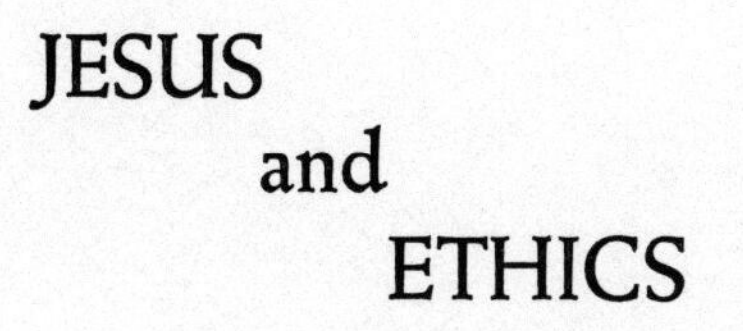
JESUS
and
ETHICS

JESUS and ETHICS

Four Interpretations

by

RICHARD H. HIERS

THE WESTMINSTER PRESS
Philadelphia

Grateful acknowledgment is made to Holt, Rinehart and Winston, Inc., for permission to use selections from *Out of My Life and Thought* by Albert Schweitzer. Translated by C. T. Campion. Copyright 1933, 1949, 1961 by Holt, Rinehart and Winston, Inc. Reprinted by permission of Holt, Rinehart and Winston, Inc.

LIBRARY OF CONGRESS CATALOG CARD NO. 68–22644

PUBLISHED BY THE WESTMINSTER PRESS
PHILADELPHIA, PENNSYLVANIA

PRINTED IN THE UNITED STATES OF AMERICA

To

J. L. G. H.

and

M. D. H.

Contents

Preface

THIS BOOK grows out of my doctoral thesis, "The Teaching of Jesus in Christian Ethical Theory as Interpreted by New Testament Scholarship" (Yale Graduate School, 1961). There I examined not only the four principal interpretations developed here—those of Harnack, Schweitzer, Bultmann, and Dodd—but also the conclusions of several other major or representative New Testament scholars: E. F. Scott, B. H. Branscomb, Johannes Weiss, Hans Windisch, Martin Dibelius, T. W. Manson, and Amos N. Wilder. To all of them I am indebted for parts of my present understanding of the subject. In addition, I am grateful to several fellow students who patiently listened to my theories and by asking the right questions helped me to see basic features which I had not previously recognized: in particular, John B. Carman, Mark F. Cosgrove, Jack L. Stotts, and Jefferson A. White. The librarians at Yale and the University of Florida have graciously and effectively supplied me with desired literature: especially Barbara Parker and J. Ray Jones.

I am most deeply indebted to Prof. Paul Schubert and the late H. Richard Niebuhr, who undertook to counsel me as directors of the dissertation. The suggestions and criticisms of each were invaluable. It will be apparent that my own conception of ethics is derived largely from certain aspects of Professor Niebuhr's understanding. Neither Professor Schubert nor Professor Niebuhr, however, is to blame for my misunderstanding of the New Testament or ethics.

The following pages are likely to be more useful and intelligible if read in conjunction with the first three Gospels, and with some of the relevant writings of the four major interpreters, such as Harnack's *What Is Christianity?* Bultmann's *Jesus and the Word,* Schweitzer's *Out of My Life and Thought,* and Dodd's *Gospel and Law.*

R.H.H.

Gainesville, Florida

CHAPTER I

The Liberal Version of the Teaching of Jesus: Ethics Without Eschatology

Adolf von Harnack (1851–1930)

CARL GUSTAV ADOLF VON HARNACK is still the classic spokesman for so-called nineteenth-century Protestant liberalism. Its optimistic theology left this movement ill-prepared for the world catastrophes that were to befall. In 1900, Harnack professed:

> Those of us who possess more delicate and therefore more prophetic perceptions no longer regard the kingdom of love and peace as a mere Utopia.[1]

Harnack, together with other liberal Protestants generally, and the "social gospel" theologians in particular, was looking for some approximation of the Kingdom of God on earth. This optimism, it need hardly be mentioned, was sadly refuted by subsequent world history. Theological forces, as well, were to batter against the relatively simple beliefs of liberalism: the names of Karl Barth, Reinhold Niebuhr, and Rudolf Bultmann represent formidable literatures and trends which have exposed many of the inadequacies of the liberal outlook. Nevertheless, liberalism has survived into the twentieth century, both among churchmen of liberal or humanistic persuasion in various Protestant denominations—Unitarian and Quaker, notably, but by no means exclusively—and also among various Protestant theologians. Some of the most important, of course, are Bultmann (whose thought bears striking similarity to Harnack's at many points), Reinhold and Richard

Niebuhr, and Paul Tillich. These men retained and developed some aspects of liberal faith, while incorporating certain Reformation and other historical, as well as philosophical, sociological, and psychological, insights into their respective theological systems or perspectives.

There have recently been several signs of a return, if not exactly to liberal theology, at least to many of the problems that were of concern to Protestant liberalism: the renewed "quest of the historical Jesus"[2]; a revival of interest in ethics, accompanied, in many instances, by a turn away from or even against dogma.[3] Harnack's writings, in particular, have been rediscovered: in the past few years, four of his major works (totaling over 3500 pages) have been brought out in new paperback editions, three of them equipped with new, appreciative prefaces.[4] One could reasonably conclude that Harnack's importance is not confined to a now-not-so-recent phase in the history of Protestant thought. If his interpretation of Jesus and his message and their significance for ethics has some limitations, it may also have some merit and relevance in our own period.

Harnack's most celebrated book, *Das Wesen des Christentums,*[5] was produced from the stenographic notes taken by a certain Walther Becker, one of the six hundred students from all faculties at the University of Berlin who crowded into seats, aisles, and windowsills in the winter of 1899–1900 to hear the great scholar lecture on "The Essence of Christianity." The book stirred heated rejoinders, but it was immensely popular. Five editions appeared within thirteen months. Paul Tillich recalls those days:

> When . . . Adolf Harnack published his *Das Wesen des Christentums* . . . in the year 1900, it was translated into more languages than any other book except the Bible, and the Leipzig railway station was jammed by freight trains carrying Harnack's book all over the world.[6]

Here, most systematically, but in his other writings also, Harnack set forth his understanding with respect to the "kernel" or "essence" of Christianity. In many ways, Harnack's conception of Christianity was informed by the giants of liberal Protestantism, Albrecht Ritschl and Friedrich Schleiermacher.[7] Harnack quoted frequently from Goethe, whom he revered as virtually canonical. Naïvely, Harnack assumed—with many of his contemporaries—that "religion" and (Protestant) Christianity were one and the same, or that the latter represented simply the highest development of the former.[8] And yet Harnack was not simply a man influenced by his times, a "cultural Christian." He was a scholar of the first order, both in New Testament research and, especially, in the history of doctrine. Furthermore, he was an honest scholar.[9]

In all his writings Harnack strove to simplify the vast and complex materials of history and faith so that he could present "the kernel of the matter" to his contemporaries. But he knew his subject too well and had too much respect for truth to rest content with evaluations and formulas that disregarded the facts as he knew them. Thus his position with respect to many questions is ambiguous and even, occasionally, self-contradictory: e.g., as to whether Jesus believed that the Kingdom of God was entirely future, or in some sense also present, or even, in the final analysis, only present; whether dogma is necessary for the preservation and explanation of "the Gospel," or an entirely extraneous "accretion"; whether the Reformation recaptured the essence of Christianity, or itself preserved and promoted certain "incrustations"; whether, indeed, Christianity or the gospel ever had existed, even at the beginning, in "classical" or pure form. In treating Harnack's thought, therefore, it will be necessary to take into account the fact that he was ever groping for a simple statement as to the essence or kernel, but also ever correcting or supplementing such statements with other formulations. For example, in *What Is Christianity?* he provides more than ten *different* summaries of the essence or content of the gospel, and in many of his writings struggles again and again to express a Christology and a social ethic which are true to the beliefs of Jesus and the early Christians, as well as to his own combination of Lutheran and liberal Protestant convictions.

There was one matter about which Harnack had no doubt, namely, that Jesus' message was of the utmost importance to modern faith and ethics: "Defective it is not. . . . Antiquated it is not, and in life and strength it still triumphs to-day over all the past."[10] And it was not only the words and ideas of Jesus; it was also the "overpowering impression" made by his person on the disciples which shaped the future of Christianity.[11] Jesus was "an example of his message": "He who delivered it has as yet yielded his place to no man, and to human life he still to-day gives a meaning and an aim."[12] By "the Gospel," Harnack ordinarily meant Jesus' message or preaching, not the church's proclamation or kerygma about the Christ. This gospel, Harnack proposed, is essentially the same now as it was in the days of Jesus: "It contains something which, under differing historical forms, is of permanent validity."[13]

There were, however, certain difficulties in the way of an immediate and exact identification and appropriation of the gospel for modern times. For one thing, there was the problem of the New Testament sources: What really was said by Jesus, and what was added or interpolated by the Evangelists? Then there was the problem of eschatology: Jesus, like his contemporaries, expected God's Kingdom to come and history to end within, at most, a few years. How can the gospel be disentangled from these outdated and mistaken beliefs? But most of all, Harnack was concerned about the problem of distinguishing between the essence or kernel of the gospel and those dogmas of Greek and subsequent eras and cultures which had been formulated by the church, and had become so entwined about the gospel as to be readily mistaken for it. As a historian of dogma, Harnack understood his task to be that of tracing the origin of the church's dogmas, and thus differentiating between the original gospel and these later dogmas of the church.[14]

The Problem of the Sources

Unlike the writers of the "liberal lives of Jesus," Harnack recognized that the evidence of the Gospels was insufficient for the reconstruction of a "life" or "biography" of Jesus: "They tell us only of his public activity."[15] Furthermore, Harnack recognized that the Evangelists had their own particular concerns and purposes and that all their accounts were to varying degrees influenced by the disciples' beliefs, especially in Jesus' ascension and identity as Messiah.[16] Most of the proponents of the so-called "new quest of the historical Jesus" seem to be under the impression that they themselves, together with Bultmann, were the first scholars ever to take note of these problems or to read Kähler. But Harnack, also, had read Kähler—before most of them were born.[17]

Despite these difficulties, Harnack felt that the Gospels give adequate grounds for a reliable account of Jesus' sayings, the nature of his activities, and the impression he made on his disciples. There can be no certainty about a great many passages, and one must be prepared to work in terms of degrees of probability; but at least "there is some hope for an attempt to understand what his aims were, what he was, and what he signifies for us."[18] The best sources, Harnack believed, were "Q" and Mark. The former, he thought, had been written originally in Aramaic in the time of the first apostles and could bear the full weight of our confidence: "[It] affords us a really exact and profound conception of the teaching of Jesus, and is free from bias, apologetic or otherwise."[19] Mark, he thought, was somewhat later than Q, but still basically reliable, its writer having been a companion of both Peter and Paul.[20]

> On the rock of their united testimony [Q and Mark] the assault of destructive critical views, however necessary these are to easily self-satisfied research, will ever be shattered to pieces.[21]

Luke, also, was in touch with apostolic tradition, having been in Paul's company for a considerable time, and also through personal acquaintance with Jesus' disciples.[22] Furthermore, though Matthew was written with specific early Christian apologetic and liturgical interests in mind,[23] this Gospel, too, contains material which goes back to Jesus himself, notably in the Sermon on the Mount.[24] It is even likely, Harnack thought, that some of the sayings in the Fourth Gospel, especially those about the relation of the Father to the Son, have a basis in Jesus' preaching.[25] In short, those who wish to know about the ministry and preaching of the historical Jesus encounter serious problems, but they are not insurmountable if critical use is made of the New Testament sources.

The Problem of Eschatology

In his preface to the fiftieth-anniversary edition of *What Is Christianity?* Bultmann states: "Harnack somehow never clearly saw nor understood the eschatological character of the appearance of Jesus and of his preaching of the imminent advent of the Kingdom of God."[26] This criticism goes wide of the mark. Harnack clearly perceived the eschatological character, at least of Jesus' preaching and outlook. But, like Bultmann himself, as we shall see, Harnack wished to avoid the conclusion that Jesus' message was therefore mistaken or invalid with respect to later times. Harnack had read Johannes Weiss's little book which presented the thesis, together with a convincing examination of the evidence, that Jesus viewed the coming of the Kingdom of God as an entirely future and cosmic event.[27] Harnack thought it possible that this thesis might be correct.[28] In any case, as Harnack saw it, Jesus' conception of a cosmic battle between the Kingdom of God and the kingdom of the world or the evil one "was no mere image or empty idea."

> At the close of the drama he sees himself seated at the right hand of his Father, and his twelve disciples on thrones judging the twelve tribes of Israel; so objective was this picture to him, so completely in harmony with the ideas of his time.[29]

Harnack did not deny that Jesus held such eschatological beliefs, but he did deny that they had any important place in "the Gospel." Now here Harnack encountered a serious problem. On the one hand, as will be seen, he wished to maintain that the gospel or essence of Christianity is and always has been (though usually obscured by various dogmas) the basis of the Christian faith and ethics; on the other hand, he maintained that the gospel or essence of Christianity was, at its core, nothing other than the preaching of Jesus. In defending his lectures on the essence of Christianity against the charge that he had suppressed or effaced the original evidence, Harnack retorted:

> But they did not attempt to describe the preaching of Jesus in its original form, or primitive Christianity either. Rather, they intended to try to conceive *that which is essential* [*das Wesentliche*] in the phenomenon.[30]

But how, in terms of Harnack's position, can something be part of Jesus' preaching and not be "essential"? And how can there be anything "essential" that was not part of Jesus' preaching? Harnack did not formulate these questions thus, but he seemed aware of them in his treatment of Jesus' eschatological beliefs. In one way and another, Harnack undertook to show that *Jesus himself* did not take these eschatological beliefs very seriously, that although he thought the Kingdom of God future and imminent, he *also* thought of it as present and immanent, and therefore latter-day Christians may (and should) go and do likewise.

Basically, Harnack urged, Jesus understood the Kingdom of God to mean God's "reign" or "rule" (*Herrschaft*), not only in heaven, but also in the hearts of men. Harnack was not quite clear as to whether Jesus believed that God also governed the world or thought that the world remained under the reign of evil and the evil one.[31] Evidently Harnack understood that those who responded to Jesus' preaching with repentance were thereby freed from the power of the devil. Those who acknowledged the "rule" or "reign" of God in their hearts or souls thereby became "members" or "citizens" of the Kingdom of God.[32]

Harnack occasionally stated, without qualification, that Jesus' message of the Kingdom and the gospel were identical: e.g., "The Gospel is the good news of the *reign* of the Almighty and Holy God, the Father and Judge of the world and of each individual soul."[33] Harnack tended to equate the "kingdom of God" with the "Fatherhood of God": "Every individual who is called into the kingdom may call on God as his Father."[34] Thus, as will be noted, in summarizing the essential content of Jesus' message, Harnack could characterize the Fatherhood of God as its "main article."[35]

Since the Kingdom of God was present as God's reign in the hearts or souls of individuals, it is evident that Harnack regarded it primarily as a phenomenon of religious experience. It is difficult to say whether Harnack was more indebted to Schleiermacher or to a kind of individualistic pietism for this conception. At any rate, he did not hesitate to describe the ultimate meaning of the Kingdom of God—for Jesus, and thus for all Christians—in such terms:

> True, the kingdom of God is the rule of God; but it is the rule of the holy God in the hearts of individuals. . . . From this point of view everything that is dramatic in the external and historical sense has vanished; and gone, too, are all the external hopes for the future. . . . [It is a question] of God and the soul, the soul and its God.[36]

It is not surprising, therefore, that when Harnack summarizes the "essential elements" in Jesus' message of the Kingdom, he omits completely any reference to its future coming, and describes it, in effect, as a matter of the individual's supernatural religious experience.[37]

In a few places, on the other hand, where Harnack writes of the significance of Jesus' message for contemporary social problems, he treats the Kingdom of God as, in some sense, a social phenomenon. It will be apparent, however, that Harnack's conception of the Kingdom of God has little in common with

Walter Rauschenbusch's definition of it as "the Christian transfiguration of the social order."[38] Though Harnack is not properly categorized as a proponent of the "social gospel," he did, frequently, include love of neighbor as a defining mark of the presence of the Kingdom of God: "The Kingdom of God is everywhere present where love is exercised, selfless love that serves."[39] Those who are citizens of the Kingdom of God are subject now to the law of love, which Harnack equates with the "higher righteousness": "This reign of God . . . places men under a *law,* which is old and yet new, *viz.:* wholehearted *love* to God and to one's neighbor."[40]

The significance of the Kingdom of God, Fatherhood of God, law of love, and related categories will be examined later in connection with Harnack's analysis of the content of the gospel. At present, it is enough to note that Harnack found the meaning of Jesus' message (and the essence of Christianity itself) in these ideas. But what has happened to Harnack's awareness that Jesus *also* regarded the Kingdom of God as a future but imminent cosmic event?

Harnack urged that one should differentiate between the traditional and the peculiar. Jesus shared the eschatological views of his contemporaries. But he held another view, namely, that in his work and message the Kingdom was already here. The latter is what should be important to us:

> It is considered a perverse procedure in similar cases to judge eminent, epoch-making personalities first and foremost by what they share with their contemporaries, and on the other hand to put what is great and characteristic in them into the background.[41]

Jesus, himself, in other words, began the process of "demythologizing," by adding his "glad message" of the rule of God in the hearts of men to the crude political, nationalistic, objective, and external cosmic hopes of his fellow Jews. Harnack's own individualism, if not contempt for the sociopolitical realm, may appear in the following description of Jesus' role in the "transformation" of the idea of the Kingdom:

> Instead of the hope of inheriting the kingdom, Jesus had also spoken simply of preserving the soul, or the life. In this one substitution lies already a transformation of universal significance, of political religion into a religion that is individual and therefore holy.[42]

The modern Christian, then, may forget about the coming of the Kingdom of God or inheriting it in the future: "From this point of view everything that was dramatic in the external and historical sense has vanished." All that remains, then, is "God and the soul, the soul and its God."[43] How did Jesus manage to hold two such contradictory ideas about the nature of the Kingdom of God? Once only, Harnack implies a distinction that has become more popular with recent writers: Jesus differentiated between the first stage of the Kingdom that had already begun to be realized in his preaching and healing and in the sacrifice of his life, and the "completion of the kingdom" which would transpire at the Parousia, his return in glory.[44] Elsewhere, Harnack seems to have been content to admit that Jesus had two different, indeed, contradictory conceptions of the Kingdom: the one, "external" and traditional; the other, his own contribution, "spiritual." Jesus simply failed to perceive the opposition between them, in the same way that people in any period may hold conflicting ideas without knowing it:

> For us, gentlemen, to-day, it is difficult to reconcile, nay, it is scarcely possible to bridge over, such an opposition as is involved, on the one side in a dramatic picture of God's kingdom existing in the future, and on the other in the announcement that "it is in the midst of you," a still and mighty power in the hearts of men. . . . I imagine that a few hundred years hence there will be found to exist in the intellectual ideas which we shall have left behind us much that is contradictory; people will wonder how we put up with it.[45]

By supposing that Jesus contemplated both interpretations Harnack opens to the historian the possibility of a choice between kernel and husk. But what if Jesus did not have both interpretations in mind, but only the dramatic, eschatological one? It evidently did not occur to Harnack that the spiritual interpretation of the Kingdom of God as God's rule in the hearts of men might be only a modern (nineteenth-century) construct.

The Problem of the Essence or the Kernel

The problem of eschatology was only part of a more fundamental problem as Harnack perceived it, namely, that of distinguishing between "the essential," i.e., "what is of permanent value" in Christianity, and the differing "co-efficients" or "historical forms" under which it has appeared.[46] The "Christian religion" or gospel, Harnack urged repeatedly, was "something simple" that "cannot easily be mistaken."[47] The trouble, however, is that the Gospel has a way of appearing in combination with various dogmas or teachings of the church. These dogmas are often mistaken for the gospel. If one is to understand the essence of Christianity, he must differentiate between the gospel and the church's dogmas.

The task of distinguishing between the gospel and the dogmas, formulas, or coefficients that have grown up with it is not to be entrusted to just anyone. Particularly, it is not to be entrusted to the fanatic, the philosopher, the antiquarian, or the apologist: the philosopher usually turns out to be a dogmatist who wishes to import some preconceived meaning into his findings; the antiquarian, if not a disguised romantic, is indifferent; and the apologist confuses historical truth with the defense and promotion of Christianity, often in the form of "some church programme of yesterday."[48] Again and again, especially in successive prefaces to *What Is Christianity?* Harnack insisted that the task in question was "purely historical," and should be undertaken only by the historian.[49] The historian, presumably, was without presuppositions, other than his concern to arrive at the truth. Harnack promises, then, that he will "keep to the purely historical theme: What is the Christian religion?"[50]

At this point, a series of ambiguities appear in Harnack's

treatment of the history of the gospel—ambiguities which best can be explained as resulting from the conflict between Harnack's desire to present the "simple" essence of Christianity, so that all who read could understand, and his honesty in dealing with the complexity of the evidence.

One of these ambiguities has to do with the question whether the gospel itself ever appeared, historically, in its pure form, i.e., apart from Jewish, Greek, or other dogmas and formularies. On the one hand, Harnack affirms that it did: it "had its classical epoch" in the teaching and person of its "founder."[51] On the other hand, Harnack can refer to the Jewish (nationalistic and apocalyptic) concepts that are found in Jesus' own preaching as "husk," and declare that none of the forms in which the gospel has appeared can be regarded as its "classical" manifestation, not even in the first.[52]

Similarly, Harnack's treatment of the Protestant Reformation is obscure with respect to this point. On the one hand, he makes the remarkable statement that in the Reformation

> religion was here brought back again to itself, in so far as the Gospel and the corresponding religious experience were put into the foreground and freed of *all* alien accretions.[53]

So completely did Harnack identify the Protestant Reformation with the original gospel that he brought his *History of Dogma* to a close with a sketch of the position of the Reformers (namely, Luther). From the original gospel to its recovery at the hands of the Reformers, "the history of dogmas can be treated as relatively a completed discipline."[54] There was nothing more to be added. And yet, Harnack admitted that "the Reformation was far from being a finished product," that Luther was incapable of distinguishing between "kernel and husk," i.e., "between 'doctrine' and 'Gospel,' " and retained much of the old dogma which he mistook for the essence of faith.[55] He also noted the "paradoxical" but "unmistakable" fact "that dogma as such is nowhere at this moment so powerful as in the Protestant Churches, though by their history they are furthest removed from it."[56] This being the case, it is understandable that Harnack wished to state, for the benefit of his own generation of Protestants, what the essence of Christianity really was. It is not clear how Harnack related his own work in doing so to that of the Reformers: whether he saw his task to be that of returning to the essence of Christianity as they had rewon it, or going beyond and completing their work by restoring the gospel to its original essence. But it is evident that he supposed that what he was presenting to his contemporaries was not merely his own liberal Protestant conception of the gospel, but the thing itself. He was no apologist or philosopher, but a *historian.* And yet, Harnack conceded that it was not possible for the gospel to "have its classical manifestation in any form of its intellectual or social types."[57] Did he mean to make an exception of the very last—the form in which he himself presented its essence to his contemporaries? How does the historian, unlike the apologist or philosopher, manage to be free of theological and philosophical commitments? If the essence of Christianity means that which is of permanent value, how is the historian as such equipped to discern and deal with matters of value? Harnack admitted that "absolute judgments as to the value to be assigned to past events" cannot be obtained from a "purely historical survey," but "are the creation only of feeling and of will; they are a subjective act."[58] But he failed to take seriously his own awareness that judgments other than of a historical character are involved in the process of ascertaining the true essence of Christianity.

Two other ambiguities appear in Harnack's thought about the gospel: his ambivalence as to the value of dogma, and his difficulty in defining the substance of the gospel.

On the one hand, Harnack inelegantly characterized dogma as "rubbish," a term that he applied alike to Jewish doctrines of Jesus' day and to Catholic beliefs and institutions up to the time of the Reformation.[59] Harnack's aversion to dogma, typical of other Protestant liberals of his period, is reflected in his insistence that Jesus was "a teacher without theology."[60] The undogmatic Jesus of liberal theology was soon to come to grief on the rocks of Schweitzer's critique.[61] Other terms Harnack used in connection with the dogmas of the church also have a definitely negative connotation: "accretion" and "incrustation." The term he most commonly used was "husk," which sometimes implies "unessential," in contrast to its counterpart, "the kernel," which is essential; but it also sometimes suggests a positive function, at least while the kernel is developing toward maturity. Such a positive function on the part of dogma is also implied in Harnack's image of the bark which protects the core of the tree, allowing the sap to rise.[62] Dogmas as "coefficients," whether religious or cultural motifs or world views, are necessary in order to "defend the kernel," under protection of such "alone living elements can grow."[63] Furthermore, dogma is necessary, he wrote, because religious feeling "has a quite definite content which determines and should determine the feeling. In this sense Christianity without dogma, that is, without a clear expression of its content, is inconceivable."[64]

Evidently, Harnack thought, as Bultmann was to put it later, that the Christian message must be mediated at any given period in terms of the particular philosophy that best renders the nature of existence intelligible if it is to awaken the response of faith and understanding. But Harnack himself did not advocate any particular philosophy or world view as the vehicle for the gospel in his own time. Though he recognized—grudgingly, to be sure—the value or necessity of various dogmas as the gospel's coefficients in its advance through the centuries, he apparently had no suspicion that his own version of the gospel or essence of Christianity could or should be anything other than the thing itself. From the standpoint of more current coefficients or interpretations, one can readily enough discern that Harnack's conception of the gospel was bound up with certain of the dogmas or coefficients of late nineteenth-century Protestant liberalism. To point this out, however, does not mean that recent coefficients, as such, are any more true or appropriate than the earlier ones, much less identical with the thing (whether defined as gospel or kerygma) itself. Nor does it mean that Harnack's conception of the gospel was in every respect incorrect. But one must insist, in Harnack's own words, against Harnack, and against one's own inclination to absolutize one's own at best partially valid insights and propositions, that the necessity of dogma "does not justify the unchangeable permanent significance of that dogma which has once been formed under definite historical conditions."[65]

Harnack's ambivalent attitude toward dogmas contains one final ambiguity. If, as he often indicated, dogma is extraneous to the essence of Christianity, why, in his book on this topic, did he devote more than a third of his space to tracing the history of the gospel through the coefficients of "Old Catholicism," Greek and Roman Catholicism, and Protestantism? As he treats these various movements, he typically asks, "What modifications did the Gospel here undergo, and how did it hold its own?"[66] He visualizes the history of Christianity as a continual struggle on the part of the gospel to "make its way" through the ever-accumulating accretions or rubbish of doctrine toward "the surface," finally emerging for the first time with the Reformation.[67] At any point along the way, Harnack evidently felt prepared to distinguish between kernel and husk, and to tell how the gospel was faring. But if the gospel is a given entity, which always is what it was at the beginning, the question remains, What did Harnack expect to learn or show from this history of the gospel about the essence of Christianity? On the other hand, Harnack does occasionally intimate that the gospel or "the Christian idea" itself has changed. In his first lecture on the essence of Christianity, Harnack promised not only to correct the various forms Christianity has taken by reference to the gospel but also to correct the chief features of the gospel "by reference to history." In his last lecture, he concluded: "It has become spiritualised, and in the course of history it has learnt how to make a surer application of its ethical principles."[68] Evidently Harnack hoped to learn something about the gospel—other than its survival value—from history after all. But in that case, his statements about the "simplicity" of the gospel, or the Reformation's recovery of

"Christianity as it originally was" must be recognized as over-simplifications.

One can appreciate that Harnack meant to affirm that there was a direct continuity between the message of Jesus, "the Gospel of Jesus Christ," and the later forms of Christianity. But it now seems clear that his basic approach to the essence of Christianity, tracing the struggle of the gospel through the succeeding centuries of dogmas to its final emergence at the time of the Reformation, or, at any rate, in nineteenth-century Protestant liberalism, is inadequate. This approach fails to take into account the difference between the preaching of Jesus and the beliefs and kerygma of the church about Jesus Christ. A good many Christians through the ages have been under the impression that the latter had something to do with the "essence" of Christianity. Harnack's visibly uneasy efforts to relate and even equate Pauline[69] and Lutheran theologies with the gospel or message of Jesus were not successful. Harnack was, in fact, to some degree aware of the kerygmatic and distinctive features of Paul's gospel, early Christian preaching, and Luther's beliefs, but he would not consider these as part of the essence of Christianity unless they could be construed as coincident with or grounded in the words of Jesus.[70] Thereby the greater part of Christian beliefs through the centuries were excluded from the essence of Christianity!

It should be said on Harnack's behalf that he was up against a difficult problem. He recognized that Christianity has changed through the centuries. But he also believed that there was some "essence" which was present "under differing historical forms," but not "in all respects identical with its earliest form."[71] Harnack was not questing after the historical Jesus, or even his message as such, so much as after that in Jesus' message which is "essential," or of "permanent validity." Bultmann would undertake to demythologize the kerygma, and also the message of Jesus, in order to discover, in effect, the essence of Christianity; Schweitzer was to write about the need to translate the conceptual material of Jesus and early Christianity into our own world view. In each case, it is affirmed that something is present now, which was present from the beginning, and yet in each case, it is recognized that Jesus and his message must be interpreted into our own categories, and not simply received without further ado into modern times: as Schweitzer was to put it bluntly, the historical Jesus is to modern man a stranger and an enigma. And yet in this process of interpretation, there is always the danger of eisegesis, i.e., of reading our own thoughts into the historical Jesus and then claiming his absolute sanction for our own only partly adequate representations. Probably no interpreter can maintain this distinction completely, for he is committed as interpreter to bringing out the meaning that is and was there in the evidence. If Harnack on occasion failed in this task,[72] he was not alone.

Harnack was inclined to confuse his own interpretation of Jesus' message with that message itself, and excluded all other messages and teachings from the essence of Christianity. Nevertheless, his contention that Jesus' message has a permanent validity, and is relevant to man's situation in the modern world, may be correct. Before examining Harnack's proposals in this connection, it is necessary first to describe his conception of the substance or content of the gospel.

The Substance of the Gospel

The number of different summaries of the essence of Christianity or the gospel which Harnack put forth is surprising. Like the ancient rabbis who endeavored (while standing on one foot or otherwise) to distill the essence of the Torah into a single epigram, Harnack tried to capture "the kernel of the matter" in one or, at most, three propositions. In fact, he provided two or three different three-point summaries. The most fully elaborated appears in *What Is Christianity?*

Firstly, the kingdom of God and its coming.

Secondly, God the Father, and the infinite value of the human soul.

Thirdly, the higher righteousness and the commandment of love.[73]

But *each* of these points, he urged, expresses "the whole of the Gospel,"[74] and in the final analysis, the three "coalesce": "For ultimately the kingdom is nothing but the treasure which the soul possesses in the eternal and merciful God."[75]

Elsewhere, he proposes that the gospel contains three elements: "the dominion [i.e., Kingdom or reign] of God, a better righteousness embodied in the law of love, and the forgiveness of sin."[76] Here the forgiveness of sin takes the place of "God the Father and the infinite value of the human soul." Another variation appears in which only one of the three first-mentioned categories remains:

> The essence of the gospel is [to be sought in] the preaching of the Fatherhood of God, and the forgiveness of sins, and in the solemnity and earnestness with which the moral law is here separated off from irreligious perversion, and impressed on the conscience.[77]

Generally, Harnack summarized the gospel in terms of one or another of the first three major categories. It is difficult to tell which he considered the most basic. The Kingdom (sovereignty or dominion) of God really meant, as Harnack understood it, individual religious experience, ultimately, "God and the soul, the soul and its God," and here, he insisted, "the whole of the Gospel is contained."[78]

On the other hand, he could say that "God's Fatherhood is the main article in Jesus' message."[79] Sometimes Harnack joined Jesus' message of the Fatherhood of God with his discovery and declaration of "the infinite value of the human soul." What Harnack had in mind, evidently, was that since God, the source of all values, was the Father of all men, all men could be seen to be of infinite value because of their relationship to him: "A real reverence for humanity follows from the practical recognition of God as the Father of us all."[80] Often, however, Harnack referred to the infinite value of the human soul as a general truth that Jesus "first brought to light," apart from any reference to the Fatherhood of God.[81] In one place he even spoke of "the idea of the inestimable *inherent* value of every individual human soul" which "stands out plainly in the preaching of Jesus," but in the same context, he adds that this idea is "united with the idea of God as Father."[82] The infinite value of the human soul is the basis for the ethic of love, since it locates value not only in the self, but in every neighbor, every man.

The third main category that Harnack says expresses the whole of the gospel of Jesus is the "higher" or "better righteousness" (cf. Matt. 5:20) which he interprets to mean the "new commandment of love."[83] Frequently, he presents the double-love commandment as the entire substance of Jesus' message. In this double-love relationship, Jesus combined "religion and morality": religion as "humility, which is the love of God of which we are capable," and morality, as love which is "what remains when the soul dies to itself" and "*serves*," in which function alone "does it exist and live."[84] Harnack's description of the love of God as humility, and his insistence that the double-love command is a matter of "the disposition and intention" in contrast to "all ceremonial sanctity and to all over-refined morality"[85] is suggestive of the distinction Bultmann was to draw between "radical" and "formal" obedience.

In addition to these three categories, Harnack also mentioned a number of other principles, ideas, or values (and disvalues) which Jesus brought to light or put forth in his message: "the good," "humility," "mercy," "purity," "the cross," "the possession of a God of grace," "joy in God, energy," "confidence in the Lord," "forgiveness of sins, certainty of eternal life, and brotherly fellowship," "the worthlessness of worldly goods and anxiety for the things of which earthly life consists," and the dangers of "mammon, care and selfishness."[86] But Harnack did not restrict the content of the gospel to ideas, values, and principles. He also saw Jesus' gospel as law, commandments, demands, injunctions, rules; as "ordinances which transform life"; and as "the moral call to repent and to believe, to renounce the world and to gain heaven."[87] Furthermore, Harnack described the gospel as a matter of the "disposition" or the heart: "the abiding disposition of the heart in love."[88] One of the many critics who early took issue with Harnack's account of the essence of Christianity observed, "He seems to conceive of Christianity as though it consisted only of ideas, of teaching."[89] This criticism fits many of the liberal Protestant proponents of the ethics of Jesus, who represented Jesus as "the master" or the great "teacher," after the likeness of an ancient Greek moral philosopher, "enunciating" or "inculcating" timeless truths or permanently valid principles or ideals for men to apply throughout the ensuing centuries.[90] In part, the criticism also applies to Harnack, though, as we have seen, Harnack also found the call to repentance, commands, and concern for the hearer's intention or disposition in Jesus' preaching. In this connection, it may be significant that Harnack often referred to Jesus' "preaching" and not only to his "teaching." But this criticism does not take into account another basic feature of Harnack's description of the gospel, namely, the centrality of Jesus himself. Harnack stated on many occasions that the gospel has to do both with Jesus and with his message.[91] To be sure, Harnack gave Jesus no credit for any interest in Christology: *"The Gospel, as Jesus proclaimed it, has to do with the Father only, and not with the Son."*[92] Nevertheless, he considered it essential "that the founder must not be forgotten over his message, nor the message over the founder."[93] Harnack was concerned with the person of Jesus as well as with his words: "Words effect nothing; it is the power of the personality that stands behind them."[94] In fact, he even could go so far as to equate the gospel with Jesus: "The *Gospel* is *Jesus Christ*. . . . It has its power in a personal life."[95] Harnack agreed with Martin Kähler that knowledge of "the historic Christ" was the one thing needful, but was not content to let knowledge of this Christ depend on the "image" of him that was the common property of the ordinary Christian in the pew; instead, he insisted, "historical labour and investigation are needed in order to grasp this Jesus Christ ever more firmly and surely."[96]

It is true, however, that Harnack had relatively little to say about the person of Jesus. It is to his credit, perhaps, that he did not attempt to write a "life of Jesus." But his own Christological statements are at best vague, and not particularly related to Synoptic or other New Testament evidence: e.g., Jesus "feels the power of the Saviour within him"; "Here the divine appeared in as pure a form as it can appear on earth."[97] His description of what Jesus understood by the title "Son of God" could have come directly from Schleiermacher:

> It is "knowledge of God" that makes the sphere of the Divine Sonship. . . . The consciousness which he possessed of being *the Son of God* is, therefore, nothing but the practical consequence of knowing God as the Father and as his Father. Rightly understood, the name of Son means nothing but the knowledge of God.[98]

Harnack would have preferred to discover in the historical Jesus a "Christ without mythology," without eschatology, without Christology, and even without theology.[99] Such a Jesus, Schweitzer soon would demonstrate, had never lived, except in the minds of liberal theologians and writers. Nevertheless, Harnack was at least aware of the importance of Jesus himself for Christianity, even if he did restrict his interest to the Jesus who "stands behind everything that he said," and ignore—so far as the essence of Christianity was concerned—what early and subsequent Christians have had to say about Jesus as the Christ. Harnack may have had in mind, though his position is not clearly developed, that Jesus himself continues to speak in the words that "speak to us across the centuries with the freshness of the present. It is here that that profound saying is truly verified 'Speak, that I may see thee.' "[100] However, when Harnack discussed the significance of Jesus for modern man, his importance appears only in connection with his "words" or gospel.

The Moral Significance of the Gospel

Harnack was convinced that the message of Jesus is as relevant today—at the turn of the twentieth century, anyway—as it was at the first: "The ethical spirit expressed in the gospels . . . must remain the basis and guideline of our development."[101] As we have seen, Harnack assumed that "the Gospel," i.e., the message of Jesus, is directly relevant to the human situation, once it is freed from the "alien accretions" that have attached to it. Many liberal (and also conservative) writers often seem to assume that Jesus' words could be valid "for us" only if he intended to address himself to us, and himself claimed for his teaching a permanent value, as if he had not really expected the end of history and the beginning of the Messianic age within a few years after all.[102] It is noteworthy that explicit statements of this sort are rare in Harnack's writings.[103] On one occasion he spoke of "what the Gospel asks of us,"[104] but ordinarily he seemed to recognize that neither Jesus nor an hypostatized gospel had "us" in view. Rather, the relevance of Jesus' message rests upon its own "permanent validity," and the constant nature of the human situation—the latter point first.

Harnack did not tire of repeating that man now is basically the same as he was in Jesus' day:

> Goethe once said, "Mankind is always advancing, and man always remains the same." It is to *man* that religion pertains—to man, as one who in the midst of all change and progress himself never changes.[105]

Furthermore, Harnack wished to show that Jesus meant his gospel for man everywhere, and, implicitly, at any time, thus in 1900 as well as in A.D. 26.

> I entertain no doubt that the founder had his eye upon *man* in whatever external situation he might be found—upon *man* who, fundamentally, always remains the same.[106]

Similarly, the message of Jesus, "although set in the framework of the Jewish nation, . . . addressed itself to the whole of humanity."[107] As a historian of early Christianity, Harnack was aware that it was because of the activities and thought of Paul and other missionaries of the "second generation" that Christianity in fact became a universal religion. "The Gospel was at first preached to the Jews exclusively." The nationalistic "Jewish limitations attaching to Jesus' message" were part of the "husk" which only fell away when "Paul transformed it into the universal religion."[108] Yet Harnack tried to show that it was *Jesus* who somehow effected this transformation. Jesus did so by speaking of "preserving the soul" instead of "inheriting the Kingdom," or by distilling the universal essence of Judaism, as recorded "by Mark 12:28–34—in its simplicity of spirit, the greatest memorial we possess of the history of religion at the epoch of its vital change," when Jesus drew together the two love commandments.[109] Or, perhaps, it was that by Jesus' opposing the perversions and pretensions of the Pharisees and by basing religion "exclusively upon repentance, humility, faith and love . . . he disentangled religion from its national setting," thus laying the groundwork for the universal mission and validity of the gospel.[110] Or, again, "by his preaching of God as the Father, *and by his own death*—he founded the universal religion."[111] The very diversity of these explanations indicates Harnack's awareness of their inadequacy. But even if Harnack could not establish that Jesus intended to found "the universal religion," he was, nevertheless, convinced of the "timeless," i.e., permanently valid, truth and relevance of Jesus' gospel: "I have tried to show what the essential elements in the Gospel are, and these elements are 'timeless.' "[112]

Since the essential content of the gospel is timeless, and since "the man to whom the Gospel addresses itself is also 'timeless' . . . , this Gospel remains in force, then, for us too."[113] As Harnack visualized it, the moral life or ethics consists mainly in the application of the ideas, values, and principles (or commands) that Jesus set forth to the various problems of modern life. "We need only grasp them in their purity and courageously apply them."[114] The values, e.g., of the human soul—humility, mercy, and purity—and the judgment as to the worthlessness of material goods are as true and relevant now as then. God is "also our Father" now, as he was then.[115] Jesus' commandments, to annihilate the enemies "mammon, care, and selfishness" are commands for us to obey.[116]

But how applicable are Jesus' ideas, principles, and commands in the modern world? Here we come to a final paradox or ambiguity in Harnack's analysis. On the one hand, he affirmed that the Christian ethic, the ethic of the Gospel, "still lies at the basis of every great social question."[117] And yet Harnack states quite emphatically that "Jesus was no social reformer," and "laid down no social programme."[118]

> What Jesus really opposes is service of mammon, Godless anxiety, and uncompassionate self-seeking, but not the present social conditions, and what he wishes to accomplish is the rule of God in the heart, not a new social program.[119]

Jesus had in mind the individual's soul, not the nation or economics or any other social institution. The gospel is indifferent to all earthly affairs.[120] "The Gospel is above all questions of mundane development; it is concerned not with material things but with the souls of men."[121] Nevertheless, Harnack balances his declaration that the gospel is "profoundly individualistic" with the statement that it is also "profoundly socialistic." It becomes "socialistic" at the point where the neighbor comes into view, as one whose soul is of "infinite and independent value." With his words, "Love thy neighbour as thyself," Jesus "turned a light upon all the concrete relations of life, upon the world of hunger, poverty and misery."[122] At the same time, Harnack insisted, it is a mistake to try to look to the gospel for any concrete proposals for social reform: "In what way you are to serve your neighbour is left to you and your own liberty of action."[123] But the lack of social or economic precepts in the gospel does not mean that the modern Christian need have no concern for these matters.

"On the contrary, where he clearly perceives that any economic condition has become a source of distress to his neighbor, he is bound to seek a remedy, for he is a disciple of the Saviour."[124]

If this were all, one might conclude that Harnack described the nature and relevance of the gospel very cogently. Indeed, perhaps he did so, in some respects, more adequately than Bultmann or Dodd. But there are some qualifications to be noted. Harnack, of course, was correct in declaring that Jesus was no social reformer. But he did not perceive that the Christian (or any morally serious person) who wishes to love his neighbor responsibly is under a moral obligation to inform himself with respect to the social and economic conditions in which his neighbor lives. Unlike Rauschenbusch, the Niebuhrs, and recent advocates of "situation ethics"—the last of whom at least write about the necessity of knowing the facts of the concrete situation—Harnack was for the most part content to leave these matters to the experts, or, as a good German Lutheran, to the imperial government. Though he recognized the demonic character of unbridled, free enterprise economics and the inadequacy of mere charity as a method for dealing with modern economic and social problems, he was not interested in institutional reforms.[125] Calling for a staff of trained deacons and deaconesses to minister to the needy in every parish was about as far as Harnack felt it proper to go in this direction.[126] He did, however, advocate study of "the construction of the social organism," but not in order to change that organism, rather, only to see which of its ills were "inevitable," and which might be remedied by self-sacrifice.[127] To the extent that he considered the Kingdom of God as a present social phenomenon at all, Harnack equated it with "diligent pursuit of one's calling" or the "great" and "independent" "order of creation" about which "Luther has taught us."[128]

Harnack's understanding of the political realm was, to put it charitably, naïve. He saw no value in political parties; instead, all should unite in support of the fatherland. His impassioned propaganda speech delivered and printed to inspire the German war effort in the fall of 1914[129] is a perfect example of the pathetic but dangerous illusions of the "children of light." He was convinced that wicked enemies abroad, notably England, were the sole cause of the war, and was oblivious—in typically Lutheran fashion—of the pretentiousness of claims to absolute innocence and virtue made on behalf of the beloved German kaiser and fatherland. He was sure that God was on the side of the Germans, that the most ethical nation (Germany) would triumph, and then be able to get on with its mission as cultural messiah of the world.[130] In the enthusiasm of the moment, he was well on the way to equating the coming great fatherland with the Kingdom of God which Jesus had promised would "gradually take shape and form within humanity."[131] He describes the two in identical terms: "a brotherhood as inclusive as the whole of human life, and as profound as human need."[132] To Harnack's credit, it should be added that after the war he was able to perceive the defeat of the German nation as an act of God's judgment: "Why does He destroy it? Because it lived without Him; but without Him it was not worthy to live; this is what He wants to show us through its destruction, for otherwise we would not have believed it."[133]

A pronounced individualistic, anti-institutional strain runs through Harnack's social ethics. He could insist, for instance, that

> the Kingdom of God must be built upon the foundation, not of institutions, but of individuals in whom God dwells, and who are glad to live for their fellow men.[134]

Evidently, Harnack felt that because Jesus did not advocate social reform, the modern Christian and the Christian church should not do so either. Because no "injunctions bidding us forcibly alter the conditions of the age in which we may happen to be living are . . . to be found in the Gospel," Harnack inferred that the Christian should be content to let these conditions remain as they are. "The Gospel makes its appeal to the inner man"; Jesus said, " 'My kingdom is not of this world'; it is no earthly kingdom that the Gospel establishes. These words

. . . forbid all direct and formal interference of religion in worldly affairs."[135]

This last statement leads to a final criticism. Harnack did not fully appreciate the importance of Jesus' eschatological outlook when treating his attitude toward "the world" or "material things." To be sure, Harnack urged that Jesus did not advocate asceticism or world denial as such. And yet, Harnack frequently stated without qualification that Jesus required—and/or the modern disciples also must practice—indifference to material things. Though in this respect less of a Platonist than Dodd, Harnack nevertheless found more of a metaphysical than a cosmic dualism in "the Gospel."

> The Gospel is based—and this is the all-important element in the view which it takes of the world and history—upon the antithesis between Spirit and flesh, God and the world, good and evil. . . . It is by self-conquest that a man is freed from the tyranny of matter.[136]

Possibly the notion that the enemy is matter is part of Ritschl's heritage to Harnack. What Harnack overlooked is the fact that for Jesus, Judaism, and the Old Testament generally, the world as such was regarded not as evil but as good. The distinction between God and the world is not the distinction between good and evil. Jesus warned his hearers lest they fail to make ready for the coming decisive time when those who were prepared would be called to enter or "inherit" the Kingdom of God, while those ill-prepared would be excluded from its blessings. If he called on them to renounce the world, it was not because the world was inherently evil—though he may have shared the belief that it had come under Satan's power—and it was not so that they could "gain heaven,"[137] but so that they might hope to inherit the Kingdom of God on earth. If Harnack prematurely demythologized Jesus' outlook, and mistook cosmic for metaphysical dualism, Schweitzer's studies would soon provide a needed corrective.

To the extent that Harnack recognized that there was also a moral dualism, a "dualism of decision," in Jesus' preaching, he would later be vindicated by Bultmann. Though he thought mainly in terms of Jesus' ideas and principles, Harnack at least partly grasped the importance of decision in response to Jesus' preaching: "The distinction of good and evil—for God or against God—he would make a life question for every man."[138] But Harnack did not see any connection between Jesus' call for decision and the coming of the Kingdom of God and time of judgment. It was the "glad message of mercy and the Fatherhood of God"[139] alone that was to move his hearers to decision. The essence of the gospel was an ethics without eschatology.

CHAPTER II

The Historical Jesus vs. Modern Theology: Ethics and Eschatology

Albert Schweitzer (1875–1965)

SCHWEITZER found it painful that in following his calling as critical historian with full respect for the truth, he came to realize that the Jesus who was so admired by the "modern"—i.e., late nineteenth- and early twentieth-century Protestant liberal—theology bore little or no resemblance to the Jesus of history. Schweitzer comforted himself with the recollection of Paul's dictum, "We can do nothing against the truth,"[1] and proceeded with the literary-historical investigation of Jesus and his message. He first set forth his findings in 1901 in a small book, entitled in English, *The Mystery of the Kingdom of God.*[2] This was followed in 1906 with his classic critique of the eighteenth- and nineteenth-century "Lives of Jesus," *Von Reimarus zu Wrede,* known in English as *The Quest of the Historical Jesus.* In response to criticisms aimed at these books and to further studies of the life of Jesus—for example, a series of books claiming that Jesus had never actually lived!—Schweitzer prepared a much reworked and enlarged edition of *The Quest* in 1913 entitled *Die Geschichte der Leben-Jesu-Forschung.*[3] His M.D. dissertation appeared the same year.[4] In it he argued, mainly on the double basis of his medical studies and his findings with respect to Jesus' eschatological and Messianic beliefs, against still another theory of the life of Jesus, one that had appeared in recent psychoanalytic literature, namely, that Jesus was a paranoid or some other type of psychopath.

Ten years later, two more books were published in which Schweitzer expressed himself particularly with regard to the significance of Jesus for ethics: *Christianity and the Religions of the World*[5] and his two volumes on *The Philosophy of Civilization.*[6] His most recent reflections on Jesus' life and teachings and their significance are to be found in *The Mysticism of Paul the Apostle,* his last major writing in the field of New Testament, published in 1929,[7] and his autobiography *Out of My Life and Thought,* written in 1931. The latter is especially valuable both as a summary of Schweitzer's career and previous writings, and as a clue to his final understanding of the questions with which we are concerned. His more recent, but briefer, reflections correspond in the main with the interpretation indicated in his autobiography.[8]

Schweitzer had great respect for many of the giants of the nineteenth-century "quest," such as Harnack, whose lectures he had attended, and his teacher, H. J. Holtzmann. In his judgment, Harnack's *What Is Christianity?* was the best or at least the "most living presentation" of the nineteenth-century "modern" or liberal understanding of Jesus and his teaching,[9] an understanding toward which Schweitzer himself remained *theologically* sympathetic. The problem Schweitzer found with this kind of interpretation, however, was that it failed to distinguish between the genuine historical Jesus and the theological and ethical constructs and concerns of his latter-day interpreters: "Harnack, in his 'What Is Christianity?' almost entirely ignores the contemporary limitations of Jesus' teaching, and starts out with a Gospel which carries him down without difficulty to the year 1899."[10] What the modern interpreters failed to realize, Schweitzer perceived, is that Jesus was not a modern man, but rather, one whose ideas about himself, his mission, the world, and history belonged to early first-century Judaism. Those interpretations which fail to take Jesus' own world view into account necessarily remain subjective: they tell much about the concerns of the interpreter, but little or nothing about the historical Jesus or his beliefs.

THE HISTORICAL, ESCHATOLOGICAL JESUS

The historical Jesus whom Schweitzer found in the Synoptic Gospels fully shared the beliefs of his contemporaries with regard to Satan and demons, and in particular, with regard to time.[11] The present age was drawing to a close; soon the Son of Man and the coming age, the Kingdom of God, would be here. The dead would be raised and, with the living, would be judged. The righteous would then enter into the Kingdom of God, and the wicked would forever be excluded from its joys.

Jesus differed from many of his contemporaries in his conviction that this critical moment—the coming of the Son of Man and the Kingdom of God to earth—was imminent. Perhaps he had learned this from John the Baptist. At any rate, the nearness of the Kingdom of God became the central theme in his preaching (Mark 1:15). Believing that the end of the present age was near, he sent out his disciples to hasten throughout Israel broadcasting this message so that as many as possible might have opportunity to repent before it was too late (Matt. 10:23). Jesus' so-called "ethical teaching" was not, therefore, laid down or "inculcated" as timeless truths intended for the guidance of the moral life of countless generations to come. Instead, Jesus' teaching was, in the expression Schweitzer coined in *The Mystery of the Kingdom of God,* an "interim ethic" or "ethic for the interim" between his (and his disciples') preaching and the coming of the Kingdom of God and the Son of Man. The Beatitudes and parables all have the same theme: by repentance, meaning moral renewal or transformation, one must now prepare for the one thing that matters—the coming of the Kingdom of God. Following the moral life indicated in Jesus' instructions makes "one meet for the Kingdom of God."[12] "Whosoever at the dawning of the Kingdom is in possession of a character morally renovated will be found a member of the same."[13] Schweitzer was aware that his characterization of Jesus' ethical teaching as an interim ethic meant that it was now no longer possible to view Jesus' teaching as intended by him for our time. Nor do we any longer expect the Kingdom of God to appear in the near future. What, then, is the significance, if any, of Jesus' teaching in our day? Schweitzer was very much concerned about this question, and, as we shall see, responded to it with a number of different answers.

Jesus also differed from his contemporaries in one other and decisive respect. Jesus understood himself to be the one who would soon be revealed as the Christ. Nineteenth-century liberals, as we have seen in the case of Harnack, preferred to think of Jesus only in some vague or highly qualified sense as "Christ." They were not, in general, open to the evidence that Jesus conceived at least his future role as that of the Christ or Messiah. While scarcely an advocate of any of the traditional dogmatic Christologies, Schweitzer does not shrink from attributing to Jesus a particular consciousness of his Messiahship. But Schweitzer believed that the thesis of the "Messianic secret" in Mark is historically correct: Jesus did not announce his identity publicly, much less require of his contemporaries belief in himself as Messiah. Jesus kept the secret of his Messiahship well, for "during the whole of his Galilean ministry the people knew no more than that he was a prophet or Elijah."[14]

Jesus knew that he, himself, would come as Son of Man or Messiah. He did not believe it necessary to proclaim this in public, however, since he soon would be revealed as such. Instead, Jesus spoke of the coming of the Son of Man as if the latter were someone other than himself. But he also, in many sayings, "suggested the *absolute solidarity* between himself and the Son of man whom he proclaimed."[15] By acknowledging his authority, and through fellowship with him, Jesus' followers enter into fellowship— though they do not yet realize it[16]— with the coming Son of Man, and are, thus, sacramentally set apart for salvation on the day when the Son of Man shall sit in judgment:

Without revealing to His hearers the content of His own self-consciousness, He brings [his followers] again and again face to face with the thought that by fellowship with Him they have fellowship with the Son of man.[17]

This "mysticism" or fellowship with himself is really "Christ mysticism," but he offers it to his hearers as a mystery, for they do not know that it is he, himself, who will come as the Christ or Son of Man. When his identity is revealed, "there will be some great surprises in the Day of Judgment" for those who have previously shared or declined fellowship with him.[18]

There is yet another "mystery" or secret in Jesus' understanding of his mission or role. Initially, Jesus had expected that the Kingdom of God would come soon. But before it could come, according to Jewish thought of the day, there would first be a period of final "woes," "affliction," or "tribulation" (*peirasmos*): in effect, "the last desperate attack of the powers of this world."[19] Since with God "all things are possible," Jesus thought that God *might* bring his Kingdom without it first being necessary for the faithful to pass through the time of tribulation. Thus he taught his disciples to pray that God's Kingdom might come and that they might be spared the "temptation," the final onslaught of "the evil one" (Matt. 6:13).

In his first book on the subject, Schweitzer took the position that Jesus was not content merely to announce that the arrival of the Kingdom was near and to send out his disciples as bearers of this news. He also meant to hasten the arrival of the Kingdom. It would be hastened by force of the repentance awakened by Jesus' and the disciples' preaching.[20] Schweitzer interprets the "men of violence" (Matt. 11:12) as those who "put into practice the moral renewal," and thus compel the Kingdom to appear. He infers such an idea from prophetic and later Jewish thought. In his more recent books, however, Schweitzer abandoned this interpretation. And yet, in still another way, he continued to maintain that Jesus did intend to hasten the coming of the Kingdom.

When Jesus sent out his disciples on their urgent mission of healing and proclaiming the nearness of the Kingdom of God, he warned them that they would have to endure the final affliction or tribulations of the powers of evil. He also expected that before they could finish their urgent mission through the towns of Israel, the Son of Man would have appeared (Matt. 10:23). But the disciples returned (Mark 6:30 = Luke 9:10); they had not experienced the final tribulation, and the Kingdom of God and Son of Man had not appeared! In the meantime, the Baptist, whom Jesus had recognized as Elijah, the prophet who was to come before the Messianic age (Mal. 4:5 f.), had been executed by Herod (Mark 6:17–29).

In order to comprehend this new turn of events, Jesus withdrew with his companions to a place of solitude (Mark 6:31 f.). Here, under the influence of both the clue to his own fate given in that of the Baptist, Elijah, his "forerunner," and the pattern of the Suffering Servant who gave his life "for many," which act was to culminate not only in the judgment of Israel and the world but also in the enthronement of God above a new heaven and a new earth (Isa., chs. 52 to 66), Jesus determined to accept the task now disclosed to him as his own. He would take upon himself the tribulation of the last times, and thereby remove the final obstacle in the way of the coming of the Kingdom:

> He who one day shall reign over the believers as Messiah now humbles himself under them and serves them by giving his life as a ransom for many, in order that the Kingdom may dawn upon them.[21]

Jesus then proceeds to Jerusalem in order to be put to death and thereby fulfill the last part of his pre-Messianic role. His followers will consequently be spared the necessity of passing through the tribulation with him; the Kingdom, so Jesus expected, would come immediately after his death.[22] Jesus' death was a dogmatic necessity: given the eschatological and Messianic beliefs that he held, his death was necessary if the Kingdom of God was to come and his followers were to be spared the final tribulation. Afterward, he would rise from the dead and lead them to Galilee, where he would be exalted as Son of Man.[23]

Such a Jesus is indeed no modern man! In Schweitzer's words, "The historical Jesus will be to our time a stranger and an enigma."[24] Schweitzer's study of the life of Jesus makes clear what was, for the most part, covered over by Harnack and the writers of the "liberal lives" of Jesus, namely, that there is a vast gap or chasm between the actual historical Jesus, whose thought and activity were governed by eschatological and Messianic dogmas, and the Jesus portrayed in the "liberal lives," whose life and, especially, whose teaching provided the principles and ideals of the then "modern" theology and ethics, at least for liberal Protestants.

The Significance of the Historical Jesus and His Message

One might expect that Schweitzer would have concluded that this strange Jesus and his teaching no longer have any significance for modern man. This, in fact, is what many recent commentators mistakenly suppose when they encounter Schweitzer's characterization of Jesus' ethics as an interim ethic.[25] It is quite clear, however, that Schweitzer understood that the authority and meaning of Jesus and his teaching are as powerful and relevant now as they were during Jesus' lifetime. In fact, one of the basic themes that runs through Schweitzer's writings about the historical Jesus is his concern to present Jesus in "his overwhelming heroic greatness" to his own generation which had been confused by the current sentimentalized and enervating modernizations of Jesus. Before the real historical Jesus, "we must be forced to lay our faces in the dust, without daring even to wish to understand his nature." So Schweitzer wrote in his earliest treatment of the historical Jesus.[26] This sense of Jesus' overwhelming authority in our time appears also in the famous paragraph with which Schweitzer concluded *The Quest:*

> He comes to us as One unknown, without a name, as of old, by the lake-side, He came to those men who knew Him not. He speaks to us the same word: "Follow thou me!" and sets us to the tasks which he has to fulfil for our time.[27]

In his later writings, as well, Schweitzer shows that he understood Jesus as the one who addresses his promises and requirements to "us."[28]

There can be no doubt about the fact that Schweitzer regarded Jesus and his teaching as authoritative and significant in modern times. But exactly how did Schweitzer propose to account for this continuing authority and significance on the part of the historical Jesus? However heroic Jesus may have been, his eschatological and Messianic beliefs were so different from ours, and, furthermore, his expectation that the Kingdom of God would soon come was so obviously refuted by subsequent history. What can this Jesus be to us? Schweitzer notes that this question had been continuously on his mind from the beginning of his work on the life of Jesus.[29]

Schweitzer was not content with any single answer to this question; instead, he gives a number of different answers, some of which make their first appearance only in his more recent writings. The basic problem he confronted was this: "The historical Jesus of his research was a stranger and an enigma to our times; at the same time, Schweitzer felt the power and authority of Jesus and his words. There seemed to be no connection between the historical Jesus and the Jesus whom Schweitzer experienced as moral authority for the life of man in modern times. The various answers Schweitzer offers do not relate to one another in any kind of coherent system, but in common they respond to this same basic question: How is the significance of Jesus in our time to be explained? How can the gap be bridged between the historical Jesus and the Jesus relevant to us in our time?

The Presence of Jesus in the Experience of the Modern Christian[30]

There is something in the historical Jesus, despite his strangeness, that speaks directly to modern man. In a variety of ways, Schweitzer speaks of Jesus as somehow confronting the modern Christian. As early as 1913, in his revised edition of *The Quest,* he qualified his earlier assertion that Jesus must remain a stranger and an enigma to our time:

> We have the immediate impression that his Personality, in spite of all that is strange and enigmatical, has something great to say to all ages, as long as the world endures.[31]

Schweitzer seems to have been groping for a way to describe exactly what it is about Jesus that transcends this strangeness. Sometimes he speaks vaguely of "that which is elemental in him":

> Actually, the real Jesus is easier to preach than the modernized one, if only we let what is elemental in him speak to us. Thereby he is for us also the one who preaches with authority, and not as the scribes.[32]

Unfortunately, Schweitzer did not say specifically what he understood "the elemental" in Jesus to be.

In a more recent treatment, he describes the matter much more directly, in terms of the authority of the historical Jesus himself:

> Anyone who ventures to look the historical Jesus straight in the face and to listen for what He may have to teach him in His powerful sayings, soon ceases to ask what this strange seeming Jesus can still be to him. He learns to know Him as One who claims authority over him.[33]

The suggestion that one can "look the historical Jesus straight in the face" is not typical of Schweitzer, but it says plainly what elsewhere is implicit, that for Schweitzer, the *historical*

Jesus is in some manner directly accessible to the modern Christian, or, possibly, to any modern man who will look to Jesus and his teaching for authority and guidance.

More frequently, in his discussions of the question, Schweitzer employs three basic categories for describing that aspect of Jesus which transcends or bridges the gap between his world and ours: his "personality," his "Spirit," and his "will." In his final book on Paul, he introduces still another category: mystical union with Christ the Redeemer, as interpreted by Paul, and normative for Christians of all times.[34] These various conceptions appear somewhat interchangeably in Schweitzer's writings. They are not worked into a systematic structure of interpretation, but each separately and all together represent various ways in which Schweitzer attempts to symbolize the relationships he feels between the historical Jesus and the Jesus who presents himself and his claim in our time.

1. JESUS' PERSONALITY. Frequently Schweitzer speaks of the present influence or impress of Jesus' "personality" upon modern man. Possibly this is what he meant by *"das Elementare an ihm"* ("what is elemental in him"). In any case, Jesus' personality transcends the limitations of the historical Jesus, and is capable of influencing modern man.

> Even if the historical Jesus has something strange about Him, yet His personality, *as it really is,* influences us much more strongly and immediately than when He approached us in dogma and in the results attained up to the present by research.[35]

So Schweitzer wrote in 1931. In his earlier writings as well, the personality of Jesus was seen as the foundation of Christianity:

> Christianity cannot be traced to the religious mind of the Græco-Oriental type, but is something original and goes back to the personality of Jesus, who worked in Galilee and died at Jerusalem.[36]

The "personality" of Jesus, in Schweitzer's view, is the personality of the historical Jesus, as he was perceived by and impressed himself upon his contemporaries, but also as he *is* present, "as he really is," as he "influences us." The historical Jesus with his strange eschatological beliefs returns to his own time,[37] but his personality abides for all times. How can this be? How does Schweitzer propose to disentangle the personality of Jesus from the eschatological *Weltanschauung,* activity, and self-understanding of the historical Jesus? Schweitzer tried to deal with this problem in his first book on the subject.[38] It cannot be said that this attempt was successful. Although on the one hand, he wishes to show that it is illegitimate and impossible to detach Jesus' personality from his eschatological world view as the writers of the "liberal lives" had done, making him over into a modern Protestant liberal at the expense of doing violence to history, at the same time, Schweitzer wished to show that Jesus' personality, nevertheless, is not confined by his eschatological *Weltanschauung.* His suggestion is that although it is not proper or possible for modern theology to attempt the task of modernizing Jesus, it is also unnecessary, for Jesus himself, who "is really a superhuman personality," has already accomplished it:

> Genuine historical knowledge, however (unlike the liberal portraits of Jesus), restores to theology full freedom of movement. It presents to it the personality of Jesus in an eschatological world-view, yet one which is modern through and through because His mighty spirit pervades it.

> This Jesus is far greater than the one conceived in modern terms: he is really a superhuman personality. With his death he destroyed the form of his Weltanschauung, rendering his own eschatology impossible. Thereby he gives to all peoples and to all times the right to apprehend him in terms of their (own) thoughts and conceptions, in order that his spirit may pervade their "Weltanschauung" as it quickened and transfigured the Jewish eschatology.

> . . . Theology is not bound to graze in a paddock. It is free, for its task is to found our Christian view of the world solely upon the personality of Jesus Christ, *irrespective of the form in which it expressed itself in his time.* He himself has destroyed this form with his death. History prompts theology to this unhistorical step.[39]

Jesus' personality, then, transcends the historical Jesus. By his own death, by which Schweitzer evidently means to include the subsequent failure of the eschaton to materialize, the eschatological world view was evaporated, freeing Jesus' superhuman personality for apprehension in terms of any and all *Weltanschauungen.* Schweitzer, the historian, had done his work. Schweitzer, the philosopher, now tried to pick up the pieces. He found an abiding kernel or core of reality, Jesus' personality. This personality is not bound by the manner of its historical manifestation in Jesus, but is available to Christian theology as the basis upon which a modern Christian world view can be established.

It is to be asked, however, where this personality is manifested, so that the modern theologian may build upon it, if not in the historical person, Jesus of Nazareth, described in the Synoptic Gospels. What is the meaning of "the personality of Jesus Christ, *irrespective of*" its expression in the person of the historical Jesus?

Also, how does Jesus' death give "all peoples and all times the right to apprehend him" in whatever language or philosophy they choose?[40] What controls are there to safeguard against complete subjectivism or eisegesis? What is the relation between the historical Jesus with his eschatological world view, and the world views of all peoples and all times? Schweitzer calls, in effect, for demythologizing the eschatological "myths," but has no method for correlating the historical data with such theological or philosophical interpretations as may appear. Schweitzer frees the kernel of Jesus' superhuman personality from the husk of eschatology too easily by simply saying that his death rendered this eschatology impossible. It is impossible to follow Schweitzer's logic here. It would seem more probable to conclude, as did the early church, that the fulfillment of the eschatological and Messianic expectation was still to come. It is not clear for whom Schweitzer believes Jesus' death rendered his own eschatological beliefs "impossible."[41] How is it that any and all other world views were thereby rendered appropriate or valid? Schweitzer fails to show any genuine continuity between the historical Jesus and the Jesus who is a "superhuman personality."

It seems that Schweitzer's understanding of Jesus' present authority and significance as superhuman personality is achieved only by denying or forgetting about his eschatological beliefs. Thus, in his postscript to *The Mystery of the Kingdom of God,* he seems to forget about the Jesus of his historical research, who expected the Kingdom of God to come immediately after his death, whose teaching was an ethic for the brief interim which would precede that event, and thus intended only for his contemporaries, when he declares that "that mysterious Person . . . in the form of his time, knew that he was creating upon the foundation of his life and death a moral world which bears his name."[42] Similarly, in his new conclusion to *The Quest,* he declares:

> If we focus our attention upon all that is self-authenticating in His person and His Sermon on the Mount, then all which is strange and offensive can be dealt with at our leisure.[43]

Although Schweitzer means to affirm that Christianity was and is founded on the personality of the historical Jesus, he sometimes significantly implies that the proper task of modern theology is to justify *its own* beliefs by attributing them to the personality of Jesus. Thus, he writes that theology has "for its task to found *our Christian view of the world* solely upon the personality of Jesus Christ."[44] In *The Philosophy of Civilization* he explains that it was "a necessity for the progress of the spiritual life of Europe" that the modern age mistakenly placed its new optimistic world view "under the authority of the great personality of Jesus." This was a mistake, historically, because "the world-view of Jesus is thoroughly pessimistic so far as concerns the future of the natural world."[45] But in the same book, Schweitzer proceeds to develop the theory of "reverence for life" as the basis for a life and world-affirming *Weltanschauung*—for the sake of the preservation, if not the progress, of Western civilization—and then attributes this theory to the intent and teaching of the historical Jesus![46]

It is difficult to see how Schweitzer can, on the one hand, deny to modern theology the right to impute its own thoughts and concerns to the historical Jesus, and at the same time, declare that Jesus himself "gives to all people and to all times the right to apprehend him in terms of their own thoughts and conceptions."[47] In fact, Schweitzer seems to be aware that the matter was not so simple as this latter statement implies, for in his later writings he continued to search for better ways of formulating and explaining how the historical Jesus, strange as his eschatological beliefs may seem to us, is nevertheless, "for us" the supreme religious authority.

2. THE SPIRIT OF JESUS. Another conception that Schweitzer uses by way of overcoming the gap between the historical, eschatological Jesus and the world view of the modern interpreter is "the Spirit of Jesus." This is one of Schweitzer's most characteristic concepts. It would appear that Jesus' Spirit is in some manner like or related to Jesus' personality.[48] Both transcend the eschatological limitations surrounding the historical Jesus. Both represent that which is abiding and eternal in Jesus, and thus also accessible to the modern Christian. Jesus' personality is "irrespective of" the form of its historical manifestation. Likewise, Jesus' Spirit is independent of history or historical evidence:

> Jesus is something to our world because a mighty stream of spiritual influence has gone forth from him and has penetrated our time also. This fact will be neither shaken nor confirmed by an historical knowledge.[49]

This Spirit of Jesus is not only independent of history, but it is even at points in conflict with the historical Jesus:

> The Spirit of Jesus was in fact world-accepting in the sense that through the experience of the centuries, it advanced historically to the acceptance of the world, since nothing can appear phenomenally which is not in some sense ideally present from the first. But the teaching of the historical Jesus was purely and exclusively world-renouncing.[50]

Here, again, Schweitzer the philosopher seems hard put to build with the debris left by Schweitzer the historian. The notion that any given form or quality of the Spirit of Jesus that may appear (or that someone may choose to label as such) is related to something originally present in an ideal form is not a satisfactory explanation for the presence of contrary forms or qualities. That which appears subsequently may also have its origin in some new element that has been taken into the tradition or system, some element that was not ideally or otherwise present in that tradition or system from the first. Schweitzer's statement indicates that the Spirit of Jesus and the teaching of the historical Jesus are, in fact, of different origin, since the latter, being "purely and exclusively world-renouncing" can scarcely have harbored the ideal presence of "world-acceptance." Matters are complicated still further by the fact that Schweitzer seems of divided mind with respect to the question whether the Spirit of Jesus was "world-negating," and thus in accord with the outlook of the historical Jesus, or "world-accepting" and even "world-transforming," and thus congenial to the spirit of modern (early twentieth-century) optimism.[51]

Evidently, in Schweitzer's view, the Spirit of Jesus was capable of growth and adaptation; it has vitality and is not tied to the outlook of the historical Jesus:

> It may come as a stumbling-block to our faith to find that it was not Jesus himself who gave its perfect spiritual form to the truth which he brought into the world, but that it received this in the course of the working of his spirit. But this is something which we have to overcome.[52]

Liberal Christianity, Schweitzer complained, felt that there was no difference between itself and Jesus, and that there was no problem in adopting the religion of Jesus, understood as the Kingdom of God which men were to establish on earth, as its own.[53] But then Schweitzer goes on to vindicate liberal Christianity, despite its historical ineptitude, for it has the Spirit of Jesus!

> For even if that liberal Christianity has to give up identifying its belief with the teachings of Jesus in the way it used to think possible, it still has the spirit of Jesus not against it but on its side.[54]

How is the Spirit of Jesus related to the historical Jesus? The matter is sometimes formulated in terms of a dualism or polarity: on the one hand, the historical Jesus; on the other, the Spirit of Jesus. But it is only the Spirit of Jesus that is significant for the modern Christian:

> But the truth is, it is not Jesus as historically known, but Jesus as spiritually arisen within men, who is significant for our time and can help it. Not the historical Jesus, but the spirit which goes forth from Him and in the spirits of men strives for new influence and rule, is that which overcomes the world.[55]

Does this mean that the historical Jesus has no significance for our time after all? This is not, apparently, what Schweitzer really means, since he speaks of Jesus' Spirit as something having its origin "in" Jesus, and going forth "from Him." But unlike Harnack, Schweitzer disclaims the idea that the historian or historical knowledge can isolate "the abiding and eternal in Jesus":

> It is not given to history to disengage that which is abiding and eternal in the being of Jesus from the historical forms in which it worked itself out, and to introduce it into our world as a living influence. . . The abiding and eternal in

> Jesus is absolutely independent of historical knowledge and can only be understood by contact with His spirit which is still at work in the world. In proportion as we have the Spirit of Jesus we have the true knowledge of Jesus.[56]

Schweitzer evidently wanted a Jesus whose significance is "abiding and eternal." *The Quest* showed him that the historical Jesus would not do, but, he maintains, there is a spiritual Jesus "who is significant for our time and can help it." The problem that Schweitzer confronted was to show some meaningful relation or correlation between the historical and the spiritual Jesus. This is the same problem that arose in connection with his conception of the personality of Jesus.

Since that which is "abiding and eternal" in the being of Jesus is understood to have existed prior to the historical Jesus (having only temporarily "worked itself out" in that particular historical form), and since our understanding of it is "absolutely independent of historical knowledge," and thus independent of what we know about the historical Jesus, why does Schweitzer feel it necessary to speak of the Spirit *of Jesus* at all? Presumably this abiding and eternal Spirit is known elsewhere than in the historical Jesus. But is it even *possible* to speak of the Spirit *of Jesus* if we know nothing about this Spirit from historical knowledge concerning the historical Jesus? The manifestation of the "abiding and eternal" in the being of Jesus was, in Schweitzer's theory, completely hidden. But if it is completely hidden, on what ground can it be affirmed that it was present in or connected with the historical Jesus? It would appear that Schweitzer did not overcome the dichotomy between the historical Jesus and the Spirit of Jesus. He has no way of showing any intelligible continuity between the historical Jesus and his Spirit.

He goes on to mention one way in which this matter might be better understood, but does not develop the idea: namely, that there is a special relation between Jesus' Spirit and his words or teaching.

> Jesus as a concrete historical personality remains a stranger to our time, but His spirit, which lies hidden in His words, is known in simplicity, and its influence is direct. Every saying contains in its own way the whole Jesus.[57]

Schweitzer points to no qualities or marks of the Spirit of Jesus that may be identified in his words or sayings: "His spirit, . . . lies *hidden* in His words." And yet, these words, presumably (Schweitzer himself was quite prepared to make this presumption, especially in the case of Mark and Matthew), are the words of the historical Jesus. If his Spirit is known in or through these words, there may be some connection between what Schweitzer means by Jesus' Spirit, and the historical Jesus after all. Schweitzer does not seem to feel that it is necessary to "demythologize" Jesus' sayings: rather, their influence, and thus that of (the historical) Jesus is "direct."

By speaking of the Spirit of Jesus, Schweitzer evidently intended to show that Jesus is not bound by his eschatological world view and that he is, after all, of decisive importance for the life of the modern Christian. But he fails to show that it is the Spirit of *Jesus* that has this importance, and so fails to bridge the gap between the historical Jesus and the situation of the modern Christian. In *The Quest,* he shows the futility of all attempts to produce a Jesus of history who is at the same time abiding and significant to modern times. All such attempts, he urges, have ended in eisegesis or subjectivity, because they have overlooked the importance of eschatology in Jesus' thought and life. But Schweitzer does not seem to recognize that reliance upon the theory of an "ideal" Spirit of Jesus that has no describable connection with the historical Jesus also opens the door to complete subjectivity.[58]

3. THE WILL OF JESUS. By the time he was writing his conclusion to the revised edition of *The Quest,* Schweitzer had developed still another category by way of showing how the historical Jesus is authoritative and relevant for modern man: Jesus' *will.*[59]

> In reality he is an authority for us, not in the sphere of knowledge, but only in the matter of the will.[60] The true relation to Him is to be taken possession of by Him. Christian piety of any and every sort is valuable only so far as it means the surrender of our will to His.[61]

The impact of Jesus' will upon the will of the modern Christian automatically adjusts any differences between his world view and our own. All *Weltanschauungen* contain time-conditioned as well as unconditioned elements. But the will is itself "timeless." *Weltanschauungen* may differ ever so much from one another as regards their *Vorstellungsmaterial,* but can be in essence the same if penetrated and formed by the same will.[62]

> It is a question of an understanding from will to will, whereby the essence of the Weltanschauungen is transmitted directly.

> Even that which modern sensitivity generally finds objectionable in him is no longer disturbing when he is understood from will to will.[63]

The will of modern man is capable of being influenced and transformed by the will of Jesus, despite the difference in world views. To some degree, Schweitzer used the phrases "personality of Jesus," "Spirit of Jesus," and "will of Jesus" interchangeably.[64] In each case, his intention appears to be to put into conceptual language what he feels to be the basis for the authority of Jesus, an authority that can no longer be expressed in terms of a direct continuity between the historical Jesus and the modern believer. Quite possibly this last category is the most adequate of the three, for it does not involve the hypostatization of some entity whose relation to the historical Jesus cannot be demonstrated. Presumably, in Schweitzer's understanding, the will of Jesus is the will of the historical Jesus. But Jesus' will is not confined by his eschatological beliefs; at any rate, the latter is not binding for modern man, but the former can and should be:

We give history its due and then make ourselves free from its conceptual materials. But we bow before the mighty will that stands behind it, and we seek to serve this will in our time, that it may be born in us in new vitality and fruitfulness.[65]

What is the content of this will? In 1913, Schweitzer spoke only of the Kingdom of God: we have fellowship with Jesus "to the extent that we, with one another and with Him, are of one will—to put the Kingdom of God above everything else."[66] That Jesus expected God to bring his Kingdom suddenly, whereas modern men (in 1913) expected it to come through their moral labors, does not invalidate the fellowship or unity of will.

Later Schweitzer would formulate still other ways of expressing the continuity between the content of Jesus' teaching or demand and that which is incumbent upon modern man. But, curiously, he says little about the will of Jesus in connection with these later formulations.

In fact, in his more recent writings, Schweitzer speaks instead about the will *of God*. The content of God's will, in these later writings, is love: God is characterized by and equated with the "Will of Love." "In Jesus Christ, God is manifested as Will of Love."[67] And the thrust of Jesus' teaching is that "men are to be gripped by God's will of love, and must help to carry out that will in this world, in small things as in great things, in saving as in pardoning."[68]

4. ETHICAL CHRIST MYSTICISM. In some of his earlier writings, Schweitzer hinted at still another interpretation of the way in which Jesus is or should be relevant to the modern man: through mystical union with Jesus. This mysticism is described as a moral mysticism, based on the fellowship of a common will: one's will is directed and inspired by Jesus' will or God's will of love.[69]

In his last major book of New Testament research, Schweitzer developed his understanding of Christ mysticism more specifically in terms of Pauline thought. But, Schweitzer insists, Paul did not invent Christ mysticism:

> For the preaching of Jesus itself contains Christ-mysticism. It is simply not the fact that Jesus' preaching dealt with nothing but the nearness of the Kingdom of God and the ethic to be practiced during the period of waiting; He also declared that in the fellowship with Him in which they had entered His followers had already the guarantee of future fellowship with the Son of man.[70]

This was not only a fellowship of the will, but fellowship as table fellowship and personal association. Those who belong to Jesus' fellowship already belong to the fellowship of the Messiah, though they do not yet know it.[71]

It is not clear whether Schweitzer meant to say that Christ mysticism should be normative in its Pauline form or in terms of categories more akin to modern thought. Though Paul's eschatological ideas are so strange to us, "they nevertheless carry a directly convincing power in virtue of their spiritual truth which transcends all time and has value for all times."[72] And yet, Schweitzer goes on to conclude from this that "we too should claim the right to conceive the idea of union with Jesus on the lines of our own world-view."[73] Nevertheless, the Pauline formulation seems normative, according to Schweitzer, for all Christianity:

> For Christianity is a Christ-mysticism, that is to say, a "belonging together" with Christ as our Lord grasped in thought and realized in experience. By simply designating Jesus "our Lord" Paul raises Him above all the temporally conditioned conceptions in which the mystery of His personality might be grasped, and sets Him forth as the spiritual Being who transcends all human definitions, to whom we have to surrender ourselves in order to experience in Him the true law of our existence and our being.[74]

Here various strands of Schweitzer's interpretation of the person of Jesus seem to come together: he is mysterious "personality," "the Spiritual Being who transcends all human definitions" and limitations, who is "our Lord," i.e., the Lord of our wills and our lives. Christ mysticism means, in effect, acknowledging Jesus or Christ as Lord, surrendering our wills to his, and in doing his will, experiencing "mystical," i.e., ethical union or communion with him and his will. This also brings one into union with God, as one's will is conformed and united to the will of God, manifested in Jesus Christ as will of love.[75]

Schweitzer goes on to explain the significance of Jesus' ethic and belief in the Kingdom of God in terms of Paul's Christ mysticism. Paul could not, and neither can modern Christianity, simply take over Jesus' ethic or his conception of the Kingdom of God. For although Jesus expected the Kingdom of God to come immediately and preached an ethic of preparedness for it, Paul perceived that the believer, who has mystically died and risen with Christ, is already a "new creation," in whom the coming of the Kingdom of God has already begun to be experienced as redemption. Jesus believed that with his death and resurrection, the Kingdom of God would come; Paul believed that because of Jesus' death and resurrection, the redeemed man would manifest in the world "the Spirit of the Kingdom of God."[76]

Though Schweitzer's language is imprecise,[77] it is clear in this chapter that he meant to say that Paul's conception of union with Jesus through Christ mysticism was both true to the beliefs and teaching of the historical Jesus and normative for the faith of the modern Christian. These points are sufficiently evident in the following quotations:

> Paul shares Jesus' conception of the Kingdom of God, his doctrine of the redemptive significance of the death of Jesus is founded on that expectation of the Kingdom of God which is common to them both, and in his Christ-mysticism he is only developing further the concept of the redemptive significance of the fellowship of the believers with the future Messiah, which is already present in the preaching of Jesus.[78]
> It is no more possible for us than it was for Primitive Christianity and the generations between simply to set up the Gospel of Jesus as the Christian faith. . . . No other road is available to us than that which Paul opened up. It is only

by way of Christ-mysticism that we can have the experience of belief in the Kingdom of God and in redemption through Jesus Christ as a living possession.[79]

The essence of Jesus' significance, then, as Schweitzer describes it in terms of Pauline Christ mysticism, is in the present experience of redemption, perceived as "the beginning of the realization of the Kingdom of God."[80] The experience of redemption, which Schweitzer also designates as both "the Spirit of the Kingdom of God" and "the Spirit of God,"[81] becomes the basis for the life of the modern Christian:

> Jesus' ethic of preparedness for the Kingdom of God becomes, for Paul, the ethic of redemption into the state of existence proper to the Kingdom of God—a redemption known in experience through fellowship with Jesus.[82]

Here, then, are four proposals which Schweitzer offers by way of explaining the significance of the historical Jesus, despite his strange eschatological beliefs, for the modern man or modern Christian. The first three, Jesus' personality, his Spirit, and his will, though mediated by the Gospel accounts of the life of the historical Jesus, seem also to be immediately present to the modern believer. Something of this immediacy is expressed in Schweitzer's conception of Christ mysticism, but this last, unlike the first three, is mediated to us by Paul. Curiously, however, Schweitzer speaks of Paul's role and importance as mediator of Christ mysticism, and thus of Jesus' significance for later times, only in his book on Paul's mysticism and in his brief résumé of this book in his autobiography.[83] Elsewhere in his writings, Jesus' personality, Spirit, and will seem accessible to the modern believer quite apart from Paul or Christ mysticism.

Schweitzer himself, evidently, was not completely satisfied with these explanations, for in addition, he also put forward various other ways of expressing Jesus' significance. Since they have to do primarily with Jesus' beliefs and teaching, rather than with his person, these additional proposals can best be treated under a separate heading.

The Significance of Jesus' Thought and Teaching

Just as the historical, eschatologically oriented Jesus is not completely a stranger to our time after all, so also, Schweitzer reflected, Jesus' words come through to us with meaning and authority:

> Many [of Jesus' words] which at first glance seem strange become true for us also in a deep and eternal sense, if we do not try to repress the force of the Spirit which speaks out from them.[84]

His suggestion that it is the Spirit (of Jesus?) who speaks to us in or from Jesus' words occurs at several points in Schweitzer's writings. Basically, however, he maintains that Jesus' words themselves contain a definite content. This content, he urges, was true when Jesus proclaimed it to his contemporaries—to be sure, in terms of the conceptual categories or world view of his time—and has essentially the same truth or meaning for us also, even though we formulate it in conceptual materials appropriate to our own world view.

Schweitzer defines this essential or eternally valid content of Jesus' message in various ways, principally the following: as the call to serve the Kingdom of God; as "active self-devotion to others"; as the philosophy and ethic of reverence for life; and as the ethic or religion of love.

1. DEVOTION TO THE KINGDOM OF GOD. As early as 1913, Schweitzer proposed the idea that Jesus' call to seek and hope for the coming of the Kingdom of God might bridge the gap between the historical Jesus and the Jesus who can speak to us in the present world "despite the strangeness of His language." Along with Jesus, sensitive men of today "perceive that we shall be saved from present conditions through a mighty hope for the Kingdom of God and a will dedicated to it."[85]

He goes on to make adherence to Jesus' message of the Kingdom of God the touchstone of modern Christianity:

> We possess only so much of him as we let him preach to us of the Kingdom of God. The dissimilarity of metaphysics and *Vorstellungsmaterial* thereby completely disappears. What alone matters is that the idea of the Kingdom of God has the same importance for our *Weltanschauung* as it did for him, and that we experience its force and constraint as strongly as he did.[86]

Schweitzer was well aware, however, that the Kingdom of God meant something quite different to Jesus than it did to liberal theology. Schweitzer continued to maintain in his later writings that liberal theology could not identify its idea of the Kingdom of God with Jesus' eschatological beliefs about it.

> At the close of the nineteenth century, it seemed to . . . [be] finally proved that our religious thought could without further ado adopt as its own Jesus' religion of a Kingdom of God to be founded on earth. It was not long, however, before it had to admit that this description was true, only for the teaching of Jesus as it had been unconsciously modernized by itself, and not of the really historical teaching of Jesus.[87]

And yet, Schweitzer wished to maintain that the Kingdom of God is, after all, the correct goal for our striving. Can this goal be attributed to Jesus? Once or twice, he suggests that it can be justified only on grounds of necessity: for the progress of civilization or of the spiritual life of Europe.[88] That, of course, is no explanation. In his earlier writings, Schweitzer had proposed that Jesus' concern for the Kingdom and our own could be bound together by the intensity of our experience of and commitment to this great cause:

> What alone matters is that we think of the idea of the Kingdom which is to be created by ethical work with the same vehemence with which he was stirred by the expected intervention of God, and that together we know that we must be capable of giving up everything for it.[89]

Schweitzer clearly felt that fidelity to Jesus' proclamation of the Kingdom of God can be achieved, but not by claiming that our understanding of it is the same as his, indeed, not through words or ideas at all. Rather, the connection is seen in terms of a subjective identity in manner of belief ("strong and passionate"), forcefulness of experience, or of thought about it ("with the same vehemence"). But does "vehemence" (*Vehemenz*) in building the Kingdom of God through ethical labor provide a genuine point of contact with the historical Jesus who eagerly awaited it from God? Or is the modern conception of the "Kingdom of God" the same as Jesus' in name only?

Perhaps because he felt the inadequacy of this explanation, Schweitzer also had recourse, in his later writings, to the conception of Jesus' Spirit. If it was illegitimate for modern theology to adapt Jesus' conception of the Kingdom of God to its own, it might still be permissible for Jesus himself, or at least for his Spirit, to adapt his own conception so as to make it better conform to the ethical necessities and thoughts of later times.

> It was Jesus who began to spiritualize the ideas of the Kingdom of God and the Messiah. He introduced into the late-Jewish conception of the Kingdom his strong ethical emphasis on love, making this, and the consistent practice of it, the indispensable condition of entrance. By doing so he charged the late-Jewish idea of the Kingdom of God with ethical forces, which transformed it into the spiritual and ethical reality with which we are familiar.[90]

But on the same page, Schweitzer notes that it was the fact that the Kingdom failed to appear that "compelled believers to take a more and more spiritual view of the Kingdom of God." Schweitzer was obviously torn between the desire to attribute the moral and spiritual understanding of the Kingdom of God which he found religiously valid to Jesus, whom he acknowledged as the supreme moral and religious authority, and, on the other hand, his awareness as a historian that any spiritualization of the idea of the Kingdom first begins only in the

Christian community, after its nonappearance. He knew that it could not be correctly attributed to the historical Jesus,[91] and so he would have liked to attribute it to the Spirit of Jesus, who is alive in history and in the church. But as has been seen, Schweitzer was not able to show any tangible connection between the historical Jesus and the Spirit of Jesus whom he invokes in support of the beliefs of liberal theology.

It has been mentioned that in discussing the immediacy of Jesus to the modern believer through Pauline Christ mysticism, Schweitzer had again attempted to show the contemporary relevance of belief in the Kingdom of God. This, Schweitzer understood as the experience of redemption or renewal, which enables "the redeemed man to manifest . . . the Spirit of the Kingdom of God which is in him" in the world.[92] In his more recent comments on the relevance of the Kingdom of God, Schweitzer did not again revert to Pauline Christ mysticism as the medium for our receiving the experience of the Kingdom of God or redemption, but rather spoke of Jesus himself as the one who spiritualized it for us.[93]

Schweitzer himself espoused the "modern" conception of the Kingdom of God which must first of all be "in our hearts," which then by moral effort may be extended into the world.[94] Schweitzer seems to have come nearly full circle: from the criticism that liberal theology's identification of its idea of the Kingdom of God with Jesus' was historically erroneous, to the concession that it was, nevertheless, religiously or ethically true, to the conclusion that it was Jesus after all who at least initiated the process of spiritualization that ultimately came to fruition in liberal theology.[95]

Schweitzer clearly felt that Jesus' expectation of the coming Kingdom of God has religious and ethical meaning and vitality for the present time. He struggled, in effect, to "demythologize," i.e., to discover the "truth for us" that was bound up with this expectation. But it must be admitted that he did not succeed in showing how Jesus' belief in the coming of the Kingdom of God through God's action alone is transmuted into God's rule in our hearts and the commitment of men to its extension into the world through moral effort. The gap between Jesus' belief in the Kingdom of God and the understanding of that phrase in modern theology remains unbridged.

2. THE ETHIC OF SELF-DEVOTION TO OTHERS. It is only in his *Civilization and Ethics* that Schweitzer formulated the essential content of Jesus' thought as the understanding that "the ethical is the individual's active self-devotion to others."[96] Here, as in some of Schweitzer's other writings, we encounter the distinction that Schweitzer draws between Jesus' "pessimistic" or "world-denying" viewpoint, and the "optimistic", "world-affirming" attitude of modern times. These categories are somewhat imprecise, as evidenced by the fact that in one case, in order to express his meaning, Schweitzer states that Jesus' world view is "fundamentally optimistic," although "biased by the expectation of the end of the world"[97]; but, on the other hand, that his world view "is thoroughly pessimistic so far as concerns the future of the natural world."[98] These categories may be useful in describing the world view of Greco-Oriental and Indian religion, but they do not adequately describe the viewpoint of Jesus. It might have been more accurate to say that Jesus did not expect nature and history, in short, the world, to redeem itself, or for human efforts to do so, but looked for God to transform the world when he brought his Kingdom. Perhaps something of this sort is what Schweitzer meant. In any case, though Jesus did not expect men to redeem history or nature, he did, Schweitzer urges, summon men as individuals to prepare themselves for entrance into the Kingdom of God and to do so by concerning themselves with the well-being of other men:

> His religion is not a religion of world-transforming effort, but the religion of awaiting the end of the world. His ethic is characterized by activity only so far as it commands men to practice unbounded devotion to their fellow men, if they would attain to that inner perfection which is needed for entrance into the supernatural Kingdom of God.[99]

The fact that "in spite of his pessimistic attitude towards the natural world [Jesus] proclaims an ethic of active devotion to one's neighbor" made it possible, Schweitzer believed, for later Christianity to take this activist ethic of Jesus over into its optimistic, world-affirming outlook without noticing that for Jesus, this ethic was framed in the context of "a pessimistic world-view," i.e., the expectation that nature and history would soon give way to the transformed life of the Kingdom of God.

Surprisingly, Schweitzer has only three pages on "the ethic of active self-devotion taught by Jesus."[100] Despite the fact that in these three pages, Schweitzer treats this ethic as if it were the basic substance of Jesus' teaching to his contemporaries and the essence of his message for Christianity in the modern age as well, he does not proceed to develop this understanding at any greater length, or in any of his more recent writings on the subject. Quite possibly he was not able to appreciate the adequacy of this particular interpretation because of the confusion arising from his commitment to such inappropriate categories as "world-denying" and "pessimistic world-view."[101]

Interestingly, however, Schweitzer seems to have understood since he was a young man that devotion to his fellowmen, "direct human service," was the pattern of meaning for his own life indicated by the sayings of Jesus. For this reason he determined in his twenty-first year that as soon as he was thirty, he would devote himself "from that time forward to the direct service of humanity."[102] After several efforts in this direction—to care for abandoned or neglected children, for tramps and discharged prisoners, and for various poor families—he learned in his twenty-ninth year of the need of the Congo Mission for a physician, and resolved to realize his "plan of direct human service in Equatorial Africa," in order "to serve the love preached by Jesus,"[103] as he later stated it.

At the theoretical level, however, Schweitzer preferred to formulate the meaning of the content of Jesus' ethic under two other categories: the ethics of reverence for life and the ethic or religion of love.

3. THE ETHICS OF REVERENCE FOR LIFE.[104] Schweitzer reports that from boyhood he had been devoted to the cause of the protection of animal life.[105] It was not until his fortieth year, however, during his medical work in Africa that the concept "reverence for life" came to him as the dynamic of existence and the basis for an adequate philosophy of civilization.

It seemed clear to Schweitzer that thought or reason could demonstrate the validity of the ethic of reverence for life. One becomes aware of his own will to live, and discerns the will to live present in all living beings:

> The most immediate fact of man's consciousness is the assertion: "I am life which wills to live, in the midst of life which wills to live," and it is as will-to-live in the midst of will-to-live that man conceives himself during every moment that he spends in meditating on himself and the world around him.[106]

Reverence for one's own life, or one's own will to live, logically brings one to value the life of other beings as well: "If I am a thinking being, I must regard other life than my own with equal reverence."[107]

But does it really follow that affirmation of one's own life yields affirmation or reverence for the life of other persons and beings? The will to live, as Reinhold Niebuhr has shown, is more likely to become transmuted into the will to power over other persons and beings. Is the ethic of reverence for life, as Schweitzer claimed, "a necessity of thought"?

Schweitzer was aware that utilitarianism was unable to account for its theory of altruism on the basis of a refined egoism.[108] How would reverence for life bridge the gap between self-affirmation and the affirmation of the life of others? While Schweitzer maintained on the one hand that thought, at any rate, "elemental thinking,"[109] could demonstrate the validity of the ethics of reverence for life, at the same time, he also urged that this ethic must be grounded in mysticism:

> The question of what we are to make of our life . . . can be really answered only by a philosophy which brings man into a spiritual inward relation to Being, from which there result of natural necessity ethics both passive and active.[110]

"Ethics must originate in mysticism,"[111] Schweitzer maintained, but not an abstract mysticism which seeks union with "the Essence of Being," "the Absolute," or some other symbol for infinite Being; rather, it means concretely commitment to infinite Being in its infinite but particular manifestations, and thus, since man does not encounter all Being but only part of it, to that "infinitely small part of infinite Being . . . which comes within my sphere of influence and needs me."[112]

It is evident that what Schweitzer calls "mysticism" is basically the same aspect of human experience that Tillich designates as "the condition of being ultimately concerned," and that Richard Niebuhr describes as radical monotheistic faith,[113] faith understood as confidence in and devotion to its object, that being, in the case of radical monotheism, the ground or source of Being, or Being itself. That something of the sort was also Schweitzer's understanding appears, for example, in the following:

> Reverence for life means to be in the grasp of the infinite, inexplicable, forward-urging will in which all Being is grounded.
>
> The devotion of my being to infinite Being means devotion of my being to all the manifestations of Being which need my devotion, and to which I am able to devote myself.[114]

If Schweitzer had described reverence for life as reasoning about the faith relationship between selves and the object of faith, when that object is trusted and served as the infinite Being manifested in all concrete beings, instead of attempting to ground reverence for life upon reason or thought alone, or, alternately, upon mysticism, his meaning would have been expressed more precisely. Schweitzer did not wish to abandon the hope that by the impress of reverence for life upon thinking men of his time, civilization might be supplied with a rationale for the optimistic and world-affirming ethic that was necessary for its survival.[115] However, he is not quite able to synthesize this claim that reverence for life comes "as a result of thought"[116] with his more profound awareness that "world- and life-affirmation and ethics are non-rational," i.e., "religious," or grounded in "mysticism."[117]

It is not appropriate to enter here into a general critical analysis of Schweitzer's ethics of reverence for life, worthy as this may be of careful and appreciative investigation. What is of interest for our study is the fact that Schweitzer arrived at this conception, which he puts forward as the basis for ethics in the modern age, *without attempting to derive it from the ethics of Jesus.* Whether its basis is rational ("elemental") thought or nonrational mysticism, it is developed without any reliance upon the words or thought of Jesus. And yet, so strong is Schweitzer's impression of the authority of Jesus and his ethics for modern man that he nevertheless wished to attribute reverence for life to Jesus! But he does so only incidentally and rarely:

> There was only one tiny church, the community of the Quakers, which attempted to defend the unconditional validity of reverence for life, *as it is contained in the religion of Jesus.*[118]

This is the first time that Schweitzer suggested that there was any relation between reverence for life and Jesus; here it is implied that reverence for life represents all, or part of, the substance or content of Jesus' message. The only other such statement, somewhat more restrained, is in his autobiography:

> The ethic of Reverence for Life is the ethic of Love widened into universality. It is the ethic of Jesus, now recognized as a logical consequence of thought.[119]

But if it is "now recognized as a logical consequence of thought," what does Jesus have to offer in connection with this theory which the thinking man could not discover for himself? It is significant that in his final essay on "The Ethics of Reverence for Life" (1936), Schweitzer makes no mention of Jesus. Evidently he could find no real connection between the two.

4. JESUS' ETHIC OR RELIGION OF LOVE. One might suppose that Schweitzer had abandoned the hope of being able to present Jesus' message in a way that would show its intelligibility and significance for life in the modern world. The ethic of reverence for life is attributed to Jesus, but only in passing, as a gesture of respect, and really seems independent of Jesus and his teaching. But while maintaining the centrality of reverence for life for modern ethics, at the same time, Schweitzer developed the idea that Jesus had proclaimed the ethic or religion of love, and that this ethic or religion of love is the essence of his meaning for today. The two theories, reverence for life and the religion of love, are, in effect, two parallel lines of interpretation that do not, however, seem to meet anywhere in Schweitzer's understanding. It is as if with one hand he plays reverence for life, while playing Jesus' religion of love with the other. The two are not in unison, but, presumably, there is some harmony.

This latter category, together with some equivalent phrases, such as "Jesus' ethic of love" or his "ethical religion of love," appears only in Schweitzer's most recent reflections on Jesus and his significance.[120] Earlier, there had been some hints that his thought was moving in this direction: in *Civilization and Ethics* he speaks a few times of Jesus' "active ethics of self-devotion" to others, and describes the content of God's will as "the will to love."[121] He expresses the latter idea several times in his Selly Oak lectures of approximately the same date.[122]

Schweitzer used the phrases "ethic of love" and "religion of love" interchangeably. In fact, he considered Jesus' religion to be distinguished by being ethical. "The ethical is the essence of religion," both in Jesus' understanding and in Schweitzer's own:

> In the Sermon on the Mount He lets ethics, as the essence of religion, flood their hearts, leading them to judge the value of piety by what it makes of a man from the ethical point of view. Within the Messianic hopes which His hearers carry in their hearts, He kindles the fire of an ethical faith. Thus the Sermon on the Mount becomes the incontestable charter of liberal Christianity. The truth that the ethical is the essence of religion is firmly established on the authority of Jesus.[123]

This statement is remarkable in that it vindicates liberalism not only as an interpretation of Jesus' teaching but also as historically accurate. Jesus was kindling the fire of an ethical love in the hearts of his hearers, not simply urging them to repent because the Kingdom of God was at hand.

What has happened to eschatology? It was still there, to be sure. Schweitzer did not retract his historical conclusions.

> Jesus accepts, then, as true the late Jewish Messianic expectation in all its externality. In no way does He attempt to spiritualize it. But He fills it with His own powerful ethical spirit, in that, passing beyond the Law and the scribes, He demands from men the practice of the absolute ethic of love as the proof that they belong to God and to the Messiah, and that they are predestined to membership of the coming Kingdom. . . .
>
> The error of research hitherto is that it attributes to Jesus a spiritualizing of the late Jewish Messianic Expectation, whereas in reality He simply fits into it the ethical religion of love. Our minds refuse at first to grasp that a religiousness and an ethic so deep and spiritual can be combined with other views of such a naïve realism. But the combination is a fact.[124]

Jesus' ethical religion of love was thus *combined with* the contemporary eschatological and Messianic expectation. But the combination was physical rather than chemical or biological: the elements remain separable. The essential element in the combination was Jesus' ethical religion of love, which he fitted like a hand into the glove of Jewish Messianism. This understanding is similar to Harnack's characteristic distinction between the kernel and the husk. If the eschatological and Messianic elements are so evaluated, the essential element, the religion of love, can be extracted without damage and preserved for later times.

Schweitzer insisted that this process need cause no concern, that, in fact, it has already taken place.

> Further than this, the religion of love taught by Jesus has been freed from any dogmatism which clung to it by the disappearance of the late Jewish expectation of the immediate end of the world. The mold in which the casting was made has been broken. We are now at liberty to let the religion of Jesus become a living force in our thought, as its purely spiritual and ethical nature demands.[125]

Again, we see Schweitzer's remarkable principle or theory of automatic demythologizing or de-eschatologizing at work: The eschatological expectation came to nought; *therefore* we are free to see and develop in our own terms the true and abiding significance of what was once obscured because of its connection with that expectation.[126]

Schweitzer's main contention against liberalism was that it identified Jesus' world view with its own. Contrary to this procedure, Schweitzer insisted that the original eschatological setting must be recognized for what it was in historical fact, and only then interpreted:

> And so we must reconcile ourselves to the fact that Jesus' religion of love made its appearance as part of a system of thought that anticipated a speedy end of the world. We cannot make it our own through the concepts in which he proclaimed it but must rather translate it into those of our modern view of the world.
>
> Hitherto we have been doing this ingenuously and covertly. In defiance of what the words of the text said we managed to interpret the teaching of Jesus as if it were in agreement with our own view of the world.[127]

What he urged, in effect, is a critical method of demythologizing or translating the eschatological world view into something appropriate in the twentieth century. There is an essential core, the true religion of Jesus. It was cloaked in the world view of so-called "late Jewish"[128] Messianism. It is equally capable of wearing modern apparel:

> So far as its essential spiritual and ethical nature is concerned, Christianity's religious truth remains the same through the centuries. The variations belong only to the outward form which it assumes in the ideas belonging to different world-views. Thus Jesus' religion of love which made its first appearance within the framework of late Jewish eschatological expectation, finds a place later on within the late Greek, the medieval, and the modern views of the world. Nevertheless, it remains through the centuries what it is essentially. Whether it is worked out in terms of one system of thought or another is of only relative importance.[129]

As with Harnack, for Schweitzer also there was an abiding essence of Christianity that manifests itself through the centuries in changing, nonessential forms.

From the preceding, it is evident that Schweitzer was not sure in his own mind whether this process of demythologizing, or to use his own expression, "translation of world-views," is something that must be undertaken anew by each generation or culture, or whether it is a process of evolutionary development that takes place automatically. He criticizes liberalism for interpreting the teaching of Jesus as if it were in agreement with the modern world view, and insists that *we* must take responsibility for translating it into our own world view: we cannot attribute our understanding to the historical Jesus. But sometimes he uses language that implies some sort of inevitable process:

> The mighty thought underlying the Beatitudes of the Sermon on the Mount, that we come to know God and belong to Him through love, Jesus introduces into the late Jewish Messianic expectation, without being in any way concerned

> to spiritualize those realistic ideas of the Kingdom of God and of blessedness. But the spirituality which lies in this religion of love must gradually, like a refiner's fire, seize upon all ideas which come into communication with it. Thus it is the destiny of Christianity to develop through a constant process of spiritualization.[130]

In either case, it is clear that Schweitzer conceived of Jesus' religious ethic as essentially unconditioned by eschatology, and therefore permanently valid:

> The depth of Jesus' religious ethics encourages us to expect that we can find our modern ethical consciousness reflected in it. With respect to its eternal inward truth it is indeed independent of history and unconditioned by it, since it already contains the highest ethical thoughts of all times.[131]

The essence of Jesus' ethical ideas is not, then, inextricably bound up with the eschatological form. The latter is almost accidental.

Schweitzer does not say in what form Jesus' ethic of love should be translated in our time. Implicitly, he finds both the liberal commitment to the Kingdom of God and the life- and world-affirming ethic of reverence for life adequate counterparts to it. At the same time, he evidently understands that Jesus' ethic or religion of love does not need to be translated into some other world view: "Jesus' religion of love . . . remains through the centuries what it was essentially." Here, again, we find Schweitzer struggling to explain the paradox: Jesus thought entirely in terms of the world view and conceptual categories of his time; his thought and teaching are, nevertheless, somehow authoritative and significant for our time.

The historical Jesus proclaimed that his contemporaries must repent, i.e., become morally transformed: in preparation for the coming of judgment and the Kingdom of God, they were to keep the double commandment of love.[132] But Jesus' understanding that what God requires is love is not determined by his expectation that God would soon bring his

Kingdom; that expectation was only the present context in which one must now respond to God's requirement. When that expectation was disappointed, "the mold" was "broken," but Jesus' religion of love remains. In this last proposal, Schweitzer has succeeded in indicating at least one way in which some kind of continuity between the dogmatic, eschatological historical Jesus and the Jesus who can be something "to us" can be formulated after all, even if the historical Jesus had rather little to say about "love" as such.

Critique

In speaking of Jesus' personality, Spirit, and Christ mysticism, Schweitzer evidently was giving expression to his understanding that Jesus' will speaks to the will of modern man, and not merely to his contemporaries "of old." There seems to be no direct connection between the Kingdom of God as Jesus conceived it and the social ethical goal served under that name in liberal theology. Likewise, it is doubtful whether Jesus was an advocate of "reverence for life" as such, though it is clear that he believed that the Father's eye was on the sparrow and the lilies of the field, and that an animal in distress should be rescued even on the Sabbath. If Jesus' will corresponded to God's "will of love," the basic, if unformulated, unity among Schweitzer's several interpretations may be found in his understanding that this will consisted in love of God and love of neighbor.

Love of God is expressed in Schweitzer's conception of Christ mysticism, which he attributes both to the historical Jesus and to Paul, and in his sense of the authority of the personality and Spirit of Christ. This is primarily an ethical mysticism, a union of one's will with the will of Jesus, which is one with God's will of love. On the other hand, love of neighbor is expressed in the devotion of the self to the well-being of one's neighbor, and not only one's human neighbor, but all the concrete companions in Being or manifestations of Being that one encounters. Schweitzer himself did not synthesize these various elements or interpretations, but there does seem to be some such structure of unity among them.

On the other hand, several paradoxes or antinomies remain in Schweitzer's thought about the historical Jesus and his significance. Schweitzer was not able to show any genuine continuity between the personality of Jesus or the spirit of Jesus and the historical Jesus, yet he insisted that it was the personality or Spirit *of Jesus* that lives on and speaks with authority in "our time." He insisted that there is "no other road" to Jesus "than that which Paul opened up" in his formulation of Christ mysticism, but then continues to speak about the personality, Spirit, and will of Jesus and their significance for our time without further mention of Paul or Christ mysticism. He declares that modern Protestantism was historically wrong in its understanding of the Kingdom of God, but religiously correct. He seems unable to decide whether Jesus' Spirit, his conception of the Kingdom of God, and his ethical religion of love have meaning because they have translated or spiritualized themselves, as if by some automatic and self-authenticating process, or because they have been translated by Christians of various ages into more or less valid and appropriate categories. He develops the theory of reverence for life as the basis for all modern ethics and for the future of civilization without in any way deriving it from Jesus' thought, and then says that it was "contained" in Jesus' religion. Then he proceeds to speak of Jesus' ethic or religion of love as the essence of Christianity, but without bringing it into relationship with the ethics of reverence for life. It is not clear whether his final basic principle of ethics was the ethics of reverence for life, based on reason or mysticism, or Jesus' ethical religion of love, as earlier it was not clear whether it was the ethics of Christ mysticism or the ethics of devotion to the Kingdom of God.

Some of Schweitzer's proposals for explaining how it can be that Jesus and his teaching still have authority and relevance for our time are certainly of merit. His greatest contribution toward the development of a more adequate understanding of this question, however, was his impressive demonstration of the fact that the historical Jesus had been disguised and domesticated in the benign—and also not so benign—portraits of him that were current in his day and have not altogether ceased to be produced since.[133] Subsequent interpreters who wished to describe Jesus and his significance would have to begin with the historical Jesus and his eschatological beliefs, and not simply with the Jesus of liberal or some other cultural and theological brand of faith. To the extent that the eschatological interpretation of Jesus was correct, recognition of this complication could not help but serve the truth about Jesus and his meaning for the moral life of man in the modern world.

CHAPTER III

The Message of Jesus—Radical Obedience: Ethics as Eschatology

Rudolf Bultmann (1884–)

THE MOST INFLUENTIAL figure in the field of New Testament criticism and interpretation in this century is Rudolf Karl Bultmann. His contributions have been many and controversial. Each has been the object of numerous discussions: his work as a form critic; his literary analysis of the Fourth Gospel; his hermeneutical method, including his proposal for demythologizing and his understanding of the relation between New Testament interpretation and existentialist philosophy; and his interpretation of New Testament theology. These contributions will be mentioned only in connection with the subject at hand, namely, Bultmann's conception of the significance of Jesus and his teaching/preaching for the moral life.

Bultmann at one time claimed that "almost nothing" can be known about the life and personality of Jesus.[1] He regards the Synoptic outline of the life of Jesus together with the "Messianic secret" as editorial creations by Mark.[2] Nevertheless, he is confident that "the most important sayings" can be distinguished, so as to afford a consistent picture of Jesus' message.[3] Form-critical considerations, particularly the *Sitz im Leben* of the various Synoptic sayings, suggest their separation into different strata. Sayings that on grounds of language or content "can have originated only in Hellenistic Christianity," or sayings that reflect specific interests or tendencies of the

Palestinian Church "must be regarded as secondary."[4] Even so, it is often impossible to be certain which sayings are from Jesus and which originated in the church.[5] One can, however, derive from "those utterances that transcend [Jewish and Christian] interests and express great original ideas, . . . a definite conception of the preaching of Jesus."[6] Among these ideas is "radical obedience."[7] This concept of ethics is not only basic to Bultmann's description of Jesus' demand upon his contemporaries, but also, as we shall see, is the key to Bultmann's understanding of the validity of Jesus' message for us.

Jesus' Life and Mission

Bultmann does not attempt to reconstruct the course of Jesus' life; the Synoptic sources, he feels, are too fragmentary and legendary to admit such reconstruction. Scattered throughout his writings, however, are indications that he has in mind a definite conception of the general character of Jesus' life, and even of certain specific details.

Considerable evidence, he believes, points to the conclusion that Jesus originally belonged to the sect of John the Baptist. Jesus was baptized by the Baptist, and it was the Baptist "who gave him the first impetus." Jesus' movement, like John's, was Messianic, but not political, in character. The disciples of John joined Jesus' followers, who also included a Zealot. Jesus is designated several times in the Synoptic Gospels as a "prophet," and it was in the role of a Messianic prophet that he appeared. But his life and work, "measured by traditional messianic ideas, *was not messianic*."[8] Jesus is also addressed as "rabbi," a title which "marks Jesus as belonging to the class of scribes," and "implies . . . that Jesus, being a scribe, had received the necessary scribal training, and had passed the requisite scribal tests." The Gospels make it clear that "*Jesus actually lived as a Jewish rabbi*."[9] Bultmann does not attempt to explain how Jesus' appearance in the distinct roles of prophet and rabbi is to be accounted for.[10]

Jesus gathered about himself a band of disciples or "pupils," whom he "uprooted by his word" from their homes. Jesus and his disciples, convinced that the Kingdom of God was beginning and the rule of Satan ending, "in the consciousness of their mission"[11] drove out demons and healed the sick. Bultmann does not say at this point what Jesus and his disciples conceived their mission to be, or what relation there was between this mission and the exorcism of demons.[12] Elsewhere he says that Jesus understood his purpose or vocation to be "to make known the position of man before God," to make it clear "that man belongs completely to God."[13]

Many of the nineteenth-century writers of "lives of Jesus" thought that they could detect a crisis in Jesus' ministry when he became aware that there had been no genuine response by the people to his preaching. Bultmann, too, implies such a "crisis" as the occasion for Jesus' preaching taking the "form of denunciation and a summons to repentance."[14] It is not clear, however, whether Bultmann means to say that there was one such crisis or turning point in Jesus' life and proclamation, or several, *whenever* he was confronted by indifference or hostility. Bultmann believes that the accounts of Jesus' entry into Jerusalem and his cleansing of the Temple, though overgrown with legend, contain a historical kernel:

> He seems to have entered Jerusalem with a crowd of enthusiastic adherents; all were full of joy and of confidence that now the Kingdom of God was beginning. . . . Jesus entered Jerusalem, and with his followers took possession (as it seems) of the temple, in order to cleanse the holy precincts from all evil in preparation for the coming of the Kingdom.[15]

Jesus went to Jerusalem because the Kingdom was coming, but he contemplated no role for himself either in mediating its appearance or as Messiah once it had come. He took possession of the Temple, but not to precipitate retaliation by the authorities or to claim it as Messiah. The "passion predictions," which Schweitzer considered historical, Bultmann attributes to the church:

> The predictions of the passion, which represent his suffering and death as willed by God and necessary to salvation, were put in his mouth subsequently by the Church.[16]

Presumably Jesus did not expect to be put to death, or, if he did, he saw in it no Messianic or redemptive meaning. It was the church, *ex eventu,* not Jesus himself, who first associated the Messiah–Son of Man with the "Suffering Servant."[17]

Jesus' movement was one of many "messianic movements" that were current in Judaism in his day; however, Jesus neither proclaimed himself the Messiah nor led the Messianic life.[18] Against Schweitzer and others, Bultmann considers the view "that Jesus was conscious of being the one *destined to be the future messiah*" an "escape." (He does not specify *what* it is an escape from.) Instead, Jesus pointed to the Messiah or Son of Man as "the Coming One distinct from himself."[19] The Evangelists and the church, rather than Jesus himself, first identified the coming Son of Man with Jesus, since there are no Synoptic sayings in which Jesus explicitly states that he will soon return, and since it is not clear how Jesus would have visualized his removal from the earth.[20]

Despite his denial that Jesus identified himself with the coming Messiah,[21] Bultmann feels that the church was correct in making this identification, and that its affirmation is ultimately in accord with Jesus' own understanding of his ministry.[22] During his lifetime, Jesus "had demanded decision for his person as bearer of the Word." In its recognition of Jesus as Messiah, "the Church has now made this decision."[23]

In spite of his disclaimer, then, it is evident that Bultmann believes that much can be known about the "life"—at any rate, the public ministry—and intention of Jesus.[24] Still more, all that is necessary in fact, can be known about Jesus' message.

Jesus' Message: The Word

If *Jesus and the Word* is not a "life of Jesus," it was intended as a thoroughgoing account of Jesus' message and its significance. Before taking up the question of Bultmann's conception of the meaning of Jesus' message today, it is first necessary to summarize his treatment of its meaning for Jesus' contemporaries. It will be evident, however, that in treating the historical question, What *was* the meaning of Jesus' message? Bultmann is also, indeed primarily, concerned with the existential question, What *is* its meaning for us?

The Kingdom of God; Now as the Time of Decision; Radical Obedience

Bultmann is in full agreement with Schweitzer and other advocates of the futuristic interpretation of Jesus' understanding of the Kingdom of God:

> It is *supernatural, superhistorical;* and while men can "receive" its salvation, can enter it, it is not *they,* with their fellowship and their activity, who constitute the Kingdom, but God's power alone. . . . There can be no doubt that Jesus like his contemporaries expected a tremendous eschatological drama.[25]

Bultmann construes Luke 17:20 f. as anti-apocalyptical: "The Kingdom of God is (suddenly) in your midst." The Kingdom is wholly future, but imminent; it is "dawning" or "breaking in," but it is not yet here.[26] Many of his pupils, the so-called "post-Bultmannians," repeat these expressions in the hope of finding justification for their claim to discover "realized eschatology" in Jesus' conception of the Kingdom, thereby diminishing the hiatus between the kerygma and Jesus' self-understanding bequeathed them by Bultmann. Bultmann himself, however, rejects as "escape-reasoning" the theory of realized eschatology that claims "that Jesus saw the presence of God's Reign in his own person and in the followers who gathered about him."

> On the contrary, Jesus clearly expected the irruption of God's Reign as a miraculous, world-transforming event—as Judaism, and later also his own Church, did.[27]

Jesus' expectation was not, as Harnack had thought, extraneous or opposed to the rest of Jesus' teaching and outlook; instead, "the preaching of Jesus is controlled by an imminent expectation of the Reign of God."[28] The message that the Kingdom is at hand constrains men to decision: "Now is the time of decision." The nearness of the Kingdom confronts men with the "ultimate Either-Or."[29]

> *Now* is the last hour. *Now* it is Either-Or. *Now* the question is: Do men really want God's Reign? Or is it the world they want? The decision they must make is a radical one.[30]

Bultmann equates this "decision" with "repentance": "This call to decision is the call to *repentance*."[31] Ordinarily, however, he uses the former term. He also speaks of "obedience" or "radical obedience" in connection with this decision. In every situation of human existence, Jesus demands a decision between God (or God's will) and that which, because it is not God's will, is evil. To decide for God or God's will with one's *whole being*—with one's understanding and desiring—is to be radically obedient.

> He teaches men to see themselves as called to *decision*—decision between good and evil, decision for God's will or for their own will. . . . His ethic . . . is an ethic of obedience. . . . Obedience is radically conceived and involves man's whole being. This means that the whole man is under the necessity of decision; there is no neutrality for him, he has to decide between the only two possibilities which there are for his life, between good and evil.[32]

Jesus' demand for radical obedience is the same as his proclamation that man is to decide Either-Or. By "radical obedience" Bultmann means to distinguish the obedience that Jesus demanded from formal, ritual, or legal obedience. "Jesus has wholly separated obedience from legalism. . . . For God demands the whole man, not merely specific acts from the man." *Radical obedience is willing and understanding obedience;* it is not merely submission to external authority. "Radical obedience is only possible where a man understands the demand and affirms it from within himself."[33] It is important to underscore Bultmann's definition of radical obedience. It has been missed by otherwise alert students of Bultmann's position,[34] some of whom suppose that by radical obedience Bultmann means *total* obedience or "surrender" to *God's* external and arbitrary authority rather than to *the law's*. In order to try, again, to set the matter straight, Bultmann has written recently:

> By this expression I understand an obedience which does not simply submit to the commandment on the ground of its authority transmitted through the tradition, but which takes possession of the commandment in such a fashion that it affirms of itself its demand. To put it another way, radical obedience is obedience which understands.[35]

Radical Obedience as Love of Neighbor

The decision or radical obedience that Jesus demands involves man in his relation not only with God but also with his neighbor. The demand for decision or obedience is expressed in respect to one's neighbor through the commandment of love.

> Love is simply the requirement of obedience and shows how this obedience can and ought to be practiced in the concrete situation in which man is bound to man.[36] What, positively, is the will of God? *The demand for love*. . . . There is no obedience to God which does not have to prove itself in the concrete situation of meeting one's neighbor.[37]

Radical obedience, expressing itself in love of neighbor, is the ethical expression of decision for God in the Either-Or crisis that confronts man in Jesus' proclamation of the Kingdom. Love of God and love of neighbor are joined in the "double command" of love, which "wins its full significance only when it appears in connection with the preaching of Jesus." A man's attitude to God determines his attitude toward his neighbor, so that "in loving my neighbor, I prove my obedience to God."

In fact, there is no obedience to God that is directed "immediately" toward him, "no obedience separate from the concrete situation in which I stand as a man among men."[38]

> I can love my neighbor only when I surrender my will completely to God's will, so I can love God only while I will what He wills, while I really love my neighbor.[39]

Love is not an emotion or an affection; that sort of love would be self-love, for it would be preferential. Instead, love is "a definite attitude of the will."[40] The love of neighbor that Jesus demanded is also characterized by the readiness to forgive one's neighbor. In Jesus' reply to the question, "How often must I forgive my brother?" it becomes clear, Bultmann says,

> that forgiveness is no limited duty, of which a man can acquit himself, but it results necessarily from the attitude which he is to take toward his neighbor, the attitude which knows no claim of his own.[41]

What, more specifically, does Bultmann understand Jesus to mean by love of neighbor? What is the "definite attitude of the will"?

Existential Ethics: The Meaning of Love in the Concrete Situation

The central demand in Jesus' proclamation, as Bultmann sees it, is that men decide Either-Or, for God and against any other claim, including particularly one's own. Jesus taught no rules, norms, or system of ethics. *What* a man is to do in order to love his neighbor or his enemy is not specified.

> *It is assumed that everyone can know that,* and therefore Jesus' demand for love is no revelation of a new principle of ethics nor of a new conception of the dignity of man. . . . Love is simply the requirement of obedience and shows how this obedience can and ought to be practiced in the concrete situation in which man is bound to man.[42]

Love, or obedience, is a formal demand; it contains no norms or guidance as to *what* is to be done.

Bultmann suggests that renunciation of one's own claim is the only principle of conduct that is needed. The man who desires to do God's will, he says, "needs no particular rules for his conduct toward other men; his conduct is determined by renunciation of his own claim."[43] Here Bultmann's thinking is in need of supplement or correction. Renunciation of one's own claim by itself does not lead to love of neighbor. Seneca and Harnack regarded man as having "intrinsic value," but no such evaluation, Bultmann maintains, was made by Jesus. "Jesus does not support his demand for love by referring to the value of other men as human beings, and love of enemies is not the high point of universal love of humanity, but the high point of overcoming of self, the surrender of one's own claim."[44] To be sure, Jesus taught no doctrine of man's *intrinsic* value. But did he not affirm that man—one's self and one's neighbor—has value *in relation* to God and to other men? Occasionally, Bultmann shows that love is not simply the renunciation of one's own claim, and expands its definition to include concern for the neighbor. The surrender of one's own claim frees one to serve the neighbor: "Love means the surrender of one's own will *for the good* of the other man, in obedience to God."[45] Here, Bultmann's understanding of love is essentially the same as Harnack's: "Freed from its connexion with self-seeking and ritual elements, . . . it is always the love which *serves*."[46] Similarly, Schweitzer had spoken of Jesus' ethic of self-devotion to others.

But, Bultmann insists, in the situation of encounter with the neighbor, the "crisis of decision," man has no "definite standard." He "stands on no firm base, but rather *alone in empty space*."[47]

> The crisis of decision is the situation in which all observation is excluded, for which *Now* alone has meaning, which is absorbed wholly in the present moment. Now must man know what to do and leave undone, and no standard whatsoever from the past or from the universal is available. *That* is the meaning of decision.[48]

By this, however, Bultmann says that he does not mean to exclude consideration of practical possibilities or consequences of various possible alternatives: "Decision is not dice-throwing; its character becomes plainer the more clearly the empirical possibilities are understood."[49]

Bultmann's understanding of Jesus' conception of ethical decision may be congenial to the conception of "situation ethics" held by certain American moralists, but Bultmann does not develop the implication of his position, namely, that the Christian is obliged to study society so that he may be acquainted with the relevant facts and "empirical possibilities" when decisions are to be made. It is not clear, in fact, to what extent knowledge of the situation has any real place in Bultmann's understanding of decision. He says, in effect, that man will know automatically *what* to do "directly from the immediate situation," without need for reflection, observation, or any standard of judgment.

> Whoever sees man in the crisis of decision and recognizes this as the essential of human existence, assumes that man knows what is *now* good and evil; as has already been said, he knows not on the basis of any past experience or rational deductions, but directly from the immediate situation.[50]

Bultmann evidently fears that to allow any standard or reflection as to *what* is to be done will result either in the formulation of "general ideas about the highest good, about virtues and values,"[51] or else in legalism. Neither such liberalism nor legalism would be good Lutheranism, for in either case, man seeks to gain value for himself, to assert a claim, instead of surrendering his will completely to God's will. Instead, Bultmann urges, Jesus' message is that "a man learns what God wants of him immediately out of his situation in encounter with his neighbor."[52] In this "empty space" of decision, without any reference to his past experience or to any standards, values, or norms, a man will somehow *know* what is to be done.

One might ask whether, in this crisis of decision, one should or can be completely without standards or considerations of value. In the crisis of decision, Bultmann says, everyone knows or can know what to do—what is good and what is evil.[53] But how does one know good from evil? Concerning the rich man (Mark 10:17–22) who wished to know what he must do to inherit eternal life, Bultmann says:

> Truly when a man asks after the way of life, there is nothing in particular to say to him. He is to do what is right, *what everyone knows*.[54]

But what is it that everyone knows? In this story, it is quite clear that "what everyone knows" is "the commandments" (Mark 10:18–20), a very definite standard. The fact that Jesus adds a "special demand"[55]—to sell all, and give to the poor—does not amount to a repudiation of this standard.

Bultmann does not deny that the law may manifest the will of God:

> Jesus did not endeavor . . . to create a better law, but he showed that the will of God, which *can* manifest itself in the law, claims man beyond the requirement of the law.[56]

But in that case, Jesus' hearers were not left completely "alone in empty space" to make their moral response. They had in the law some indication of the will of God, even if the former does not exhaust the latter.[57]

There is also another standard or norm that Bultmann comes close to acknowledging: the sense of the value of other persons, and of one's responsibility in their presence. This consideration has already been indicated in his recognition that love of neighbor is the content of Jesus' call for radical obedience. He writes:

> Whoever sees a wounded man lying on the road knows without further command that it is right to help him. Whoever encounters the sick and oppressed knows that no Sabbath ordinance can hinder the duty to help.[58]

Bultmann cites these situations as evidence that man needs no norms or values in the "Now" of encounter with the neighbor.

But precisely in these examples, Bultmann reveals that he has a very definite standard in mind: It is "right to help" the wounded man; there is a "duty to help," compared with which, Sabbath observance is a less significant claim. The rightness or duty of helping the neighbor who is in need rests, as does Bultmann's expanded and positive definition of love, upon the affirmation of the value of the neighbor which prompts concern for his well-being, not simply upon renunciation of one's own claims. Harnack maintained that for Jesus, mankind has "infinite value," because of the Fatherhood of God. Jesus was the first, Harnack said, to bring to light and establish as a timeless truth the value of the human soul. Bultmann objects to the idea of eternal truths or eternally valid propositions. He would prefer to say that the value of the neighbor is not a general proposition of timeless validity, but rather, must be affirmed anew in each encounter with the neighbor in obedience to God. The neighbor must be perceived as one whom, in the particular moment, I not only am commanded to help but also actually desire to help, because in radical obedience I desire what God wills, namely, that which is good for the neighbor. But does it come as a complete surprise, after a series of encounters with "the neighbor," or with many neighbors, to discover each time that God wills that I affirm the being of my neighbor, and relate myself to him helpfully in his particular situation? Or, to ask the question in other words, do I not know that I am commanded to love my neighbor, to have concern for his well-being, that there is a duty to help apart from those times in the crisis of decision when I find that this is God's will? It would appear that the commandment of love itself implies a norm which informs man in the concrete situation what he is to do: namely, that God, the source of being and value, desires man's well-being and summons each man to do what is fitting to promote his neighbor's well-being in his particular situation of need.

On occasion, Bultmann concedes that there is a standard or "principle of conduct"[59] that tells what to do for the neighbor: Jesus' words, "Love your neighbor as yourself." A man knows very well, Bultmann says, what it means to love himself.[60] But what *does* it mean to love oneself? Bultmann does not examine this question. It surely must mean to affirm one's own being, to have concern for one's own needs and well-being. Is not concern for the well-being of the neighbor implicit in these words of Jesus? Certainly one neighbor's needs are not identical with another's. In this sense, Bultmann is completely correct: one must learn *what* is to be done for the neighbor from meeting the neighbor in his particular situation. The naked man needs clothing, the sick man healing. In some cases, moreover, the needs of the neighbor may not be so obvious as that of the wounded man lying in the road. But God's will, expressed in the commandment to love the neighbor as oneself, to help him in his need, remains the same, whatever the neighbor's particular need.

In the crisis of decision, it would seem, man is not entirely "alone in empty space" after all. He may be mindful of the commandment (and his own desire) to love his neighbor, to seek his neighbor's good. Further, the words "as thyself" give him some clue as to *what* is to be done for the neighbor. But Bultmann does not seem to have decided whether love, as demanded by Jesus, is really a "principle of conduct" or not. If there is to be no "observation" or reflection in the crisis of decision, what is the relevance of the love commandment or the words, "as thyself"? What, moreover, is the significance of Jesus' demands for "truthfulness and purity, readiness to sacrifice and to love"—demands which Bultmann says are stumbling blocks to the selfish will of *modern* man?[61] Bultmann does not maintain consistently that moral decision takes place in an existential vacuum after all. Instead, he understands that both Jesus' hearers and his modern disciples, indeed, "all mankind," are addressed and informed by the words of Jesus, notably, but not exhaustively, by his command of love.

Interim Ethics

What is the relation between Jesus' demand for decision, radical obedience, his commandment of love, and the fact that he believed that history was about to end and the Kingdom to be established? Bultmann claims to reject Harnack's idea that Jesus understood the Kingdom to mean an inward spiritual experience.[62] The eschatological interpretation of the Kingdom of God he finds completely vindicated by twentieth-century scholarship.[63] However, he rejects Weiss's and Schweitzer's conclusion that Jesus' teaching is to be understood as an interim ethic. In a "certain sense," he admits, it is "entirely correct" that "the words of Jesus about the will of God are to be understood strictly in the light of the eschatological message."[64] This "certain sense" is the extent to which in Jesus' demands, "Now appears as the decisive hour."[65] Bultmann's attempt to identify Jesus' eschatological beliefs with a recurrent existentialist "Now" will be examined shortly.

Bultmann objects to the interim ethics interpretation because, as he understands it, it makes obedience "a matter of prudent rules for attaining a share in the Kingdom, rather than radical and absolute." He equates "interim ethics" with "practical rules," "relative requirements," or "exceptional commands which only held for the last short interval until the end of the world."[66] Of course, if this characterization of interim ethics were accurate, that interpretation would not be invalidated just because it would be un-Lutheran or raise a question about the validity of Jesus' "ethics" in our time. In Schweitzer's theory of interim ethics (or "ethics for the interim"), however, there is no mention of "prudent rules," "relative requirements," or "exceptional commands," though perhaps there should have been, in order to account, in part at least, for such directives as those reported in Mark 10:21; Matt. 8:21 f.; Luke 9:60 and 20:35 f. Instead, Schweitzer defined interim ethics as "repentance" (*metanoia*), i.e., "moral renewal" in preparation for the coming of the Kingdom.[67] Bultmann's rejection of Schweitzer's characterization of Jesus' message as interim ethics results both from his misunderstanding of what Schweitzer meant by that term and from his own difficulty, whether as a "liberal,"[68] Lutheran, or existentialist, in taking seriously the evident fact that Jesus really shared the eschatological world view of his contemporaries.

The Real Meaning of Existence and Its Outward Expression in the Myth of Eschatology

With Harnack, Bultmann proposes to differentiate between kernel and husk in order to show, despite the fact that Jesus' expectation of the imminent end of the world was mistaken, that there are, nevertheless, elements in his proclamation "that still retain their validity."[69] Instead of dehusking, Bultmann proposes to "demythologize," i.e., disclose the existential meaning of the eschatological myths.[70]

> Does his message therefore stand or fall with that misconception? It would be better to reverse the proposition and say that *this expectation springs from the conviction which lies at the root of his preaching.* The prophets are so overwhelmed by their sense of the sovereign majesty of God and the absolute character of his will that they foreshorten the divine act of judgement. . . . This sense of crisis in human destiny expresses itself in the conviction that the hour of decision has struck. So it is with Jesus. He is so convinced of God's will and determination, and that it is his business to proclaim it, that he feels himself to be standing on the frontiers of time. . . . The understanding of human life implied thereby clearly does not stand or fall with his expectation of an imminent end of the world.[71]

Bultmann agrees with Harnack as to what the husk is: namely, "the picture of the world that Jesus shared as an ancient man and as a child of his people and time." Like Harnack also, Bultmann believes that the kernel has to do with "the idea of God, his view of man, and his relation to God, that is contained in Jesus' eschatological message." In addition, Bultmann understands the kernel to include Jesus' view of the "Now," the "hour of his appearance." What is its meaning, Bultmann asks, granting that for Jesus "the meaning of this now would naturally be objectified in the garments of a passing cosmology?"[72]

It is important to see how Bultmann conceives of Jesus' understanding of the "Now." This *now* is not something added to Jesus' idea of God and man and their relationship, but it is in the *now* that God and man encounter each other.

> The one concern in this [Jesus'] teaching was that man should conceive his immediate concrete situation as the decision to which he is constrained, and should decide in this moment for God and surrender his natural will. Just this is what we found to be *the final significance of the eschatological message,* that man *now* stands under the necessity of decision, *that his "Now" is always for him the last hour,* in which his decision against the world for God is demanded, in which every claim of his own is to be silenced.[73]

"Now" meant—so Bultmann says Jesus understood it—not only the particular moment in which he addressed a particular hearer, but every *now* or moment or concrete situation in the life of his hearers. The central point for Jesus was not the "mythological" idea that the world was about to end; this "mythology" was only the form or "garments" in which "the real meaning in Jesus' teaching finds its outward expression."[74]

Sometimes Bultmann describes this "real meaning" in terms of Jesus' "conception of man," or his "understanding of human life" or "existence."[75] By human existence, Bultmann means man in his relation to God and to his fellowmen, and particularly, the *now* in which God "meets each man in his own little history," in which man is "guided into his concrete encounter with his neighbor, in which he finds his true history."[76] Jesus was primarily concerned with human existence, with man in the "crisis of decision" before God, which crisis is "the essential characteristic" of humanity. In fact, Bultmann implies, Jesus was first an existentialist, and only afterward an eschatologist:

> Because Jesus sees man thus in a crisis of decision before God, it is understandable that in his thought the Jewish Messianic hope becomes the absolute certainty that in this

hour the Kingdom of God is coming. If men are standing in the crisis of decision, and if precisely this crisis is the essential characteristic of their humanity, then every hour is the last hour, and we can understand that for Jesus the whole contemporary mythology is pressed into the service of this conception of human existence. Thus he understood and proclaimed his hour as the last hour.[77]

Because of "contemporary mythology"—the eschatological ideas Jesus shared with his contemporaries—Jesus understood and proclaimed his particular hour as the last hour. But he was expressing thereby his *real* understanding of human existence, namely, that *every* hour is the last hour. The now is a *recurrent now* in the life of each man, as he is confronted again and again by God in encounter with his neighbor.[78] Harnack had spoken of the "timeless" validity of Jesus' words; for Bultmann, the words are not timeless, but at least implicitly, Jesus' understanding that each man is confronted with a recurrent now, that his existence is a continual crisis of decision, is timeless, i.e., still valid.

A few questions suggest themselves at this point. If Jesus genuinely shared the eschatological mythology of his contemporaries,[79] what becomes of Bultmann's proposal that Jesus was an eschatologist *because* of his sense of the crisis in human destiny in the face of the absolute claim of God's will?[80] How can he both have learned this mythology from his contemporaries *and* have derived it from his convictions about human existence? Would it not be more exact to say that, given the certainty of the coming of the Kingdom which he shared with his contemporaries, and his understanding of the radical character of the will of God, Jesus sought to prepare men for this impending crisis by demanding repentance or radical obedience to God's will? Is it true that Jesus began with "his conviction that even in the present man stands in the crisis of decision, that the present is for him the last hour," and that this "real meaning" then found "outward expression" in the view that the end of the world is at hand?[81] Is it not more likely that the crisis of decision was occasioned by belief that the

Kingdom was *in fact* at hand? Did Jesus think that the now of decision was continually recurrent for his hearers because such is the essential characteristic of human existence,[82] or because the Son of Man was coming "at an hour you do not expect"?[83] The now recurs in each encounter with the neighbor, but the now was also significant because there was little time left until men would be judged according to their obedience or faithlessness in their life in the world.[84] Jesus' understanding of "human existence" was expressed *in* his understanding that the Kingdom was at hand and in his understanding of the kind of response that was fitting because of the nearness of the Kingdom and the radical character of God's will. But it is not apparent that his understanding of human existence was conceived apart from or prior to his eschatological beliefs. In the final analysis, Bultmann, like Harnack, reduces eschatology to religious (albeit, existential) experience: "The only true interpretation of eschatology is one which makes it a real experience of human life."[85] That being the case, it is not surprising that Bultmann has difficulty understanding that Jesus' expectation of the coming Kingdom and judgment was really the context for his "ethics."

The Problem of "Reward"

Bultmann feels that certain of Jesus' sayings have no relation to his eschatological beliefs.

> It is significant that neither the imperatives of the Sermon on the Mount nor the criticisms of the Law are motivated by a reference to the judgement. There is nothing, for instance, like the Old Testament "Do this and ye shall be saved."[86]
>
> Hypocrisy is rebuked without threat of hell fire; love of enemies is demanded without the promise of heavenly joys.[87]

Bultmann concedes, however, that Jesus' proclamation as a whole was a warning to men to make ready for the coming of the Kingdom.[88] Bultmann understands Jesus' proclamation as a call to decision, an Either-Or. Only those who decide for

God will enter the Kingdom: "If men would enter the kingdom of God, they must be ready for any sacrifice."[89]

> The unity of the eschatological and the ethical message of Jesus may be so stated: Fulfilment of God's will is the *condition for participation* in the salvation of His Reign.[90]

Bultmann rejects the idea, which he identifies with the interim ethics theory, that this "condition" is to be "taken in the external sense of an arbitrarily set task."[91] Instead, he insists,

> the fulfilment of God's will is the condition for participation in the salvation of God's Reign in *this* sense, that it means nothing else but true readiness for it, genuine and earnest desire for it.

This condition is to be fulfilled by nothing other than "radical obedience."[92] Jesus believed that men would be judged according to their response to his demand for decision in the form of radical obedience.

> The judgement he speaks of is the judgement of the individual. Everyone must stand before God's tribunal and give an account of himself.[93]
>
> Jesus sees man as standing here and now under the necessity of decision, with the possibility of decision through his own free act. Only what a man now does gives him his value.[94]

Bultmann sees Jesus' idea of "reward" in a "peculiarly paradoxical, perhaps contradictory, relation to the demand for obedience."

> It is absolutely clear that Jesus demanded obedience without any secondary motive. . . . But Jesus is wholly certain that man *does* receive reward or punishment from God. . . . Jesus' attitude is indeed paradoxical; he promises reward to those who are obedient without thought of reward.
>
> But the idea of reward he holds firmly. Here too, he recognizes only an Either-Or; either reward from man or reward from God, but reward awaits every right action.[95]

But is this understanding really contradictory or paradoxical? As Bultmann himself says, it is a matter of Either-Or; men are to decide whether they desire participation in the Kingdom or some earthly (and ephemeral) treasure or satisfaction. Bultmann points out quite properly that admission to the Kingdom is not earned or deserved: "According to Jesus' view, man does not win value for himself, but if he is obedient God rewards him, gives him more than he has."[96] Nevertheless, Bultmann is dissatisfied with the answer that "the fulfilling of the will of God, obedience, is the *condition* for participation in the Kingdom, for entrance into it," for "participation in the Kingdom of God might appear as the reward sought by obedience, and thus the radical character of obedience would be lost."[97] Such a result, of course, would pose difficulties for Bultmann as a Lutheran moralist.

But was the question as to the legitimacy of the motive of reward a problem for Jesus and his hearers? If Jesus actually believed that the Kingdom of God was coming, even now breaking in, as Bultmann says he did, then the Kingdom of God and men's response to its nearness would necessarily have been his dominant concern. It would not have been a question of seeking a reward, but of being ready for this decisive and catastrophic event, which would bring the time of blessing and deliverance only for those who had made ready for it. Jesus could only have assumed that his hearers, if they believed his message, would desire a share in the Kingdom. Bultmann's view that Jesus' words are self-contradictory in that he "does occasionally use the *idea of recompense* as motivation for a demand"[98] betrays a perspective alien to Jesus' expectation of the coming Kingdom and judgment. Bultmann's proposed resolution of the problem likewise betrays a modernizing (existentializing) interest:

> Still the contradiction can probably be resolved in this way: The motive of reward is only *a primitive expression* for the idea that in what a man does *his own real being is at stake—that self which he not already is, but is to become. To achieve that self* is the legitimate motive of his ethical deal-

> ing and of his true obedience, in which he becomes aware of the paradoxical truth that *in order to arrive at himself* he must surrender to the demand of God—or, in other words, that in such surrender *he wins himself*.[99]

Was Jesus concerned that his hearers should arrive at themselves, or that they should survive the coming catastrophe and be received into the Kingdom of God?[100]

Here, as in the case of his interpretation of the relation between Jesus' belief in the nearness of the Kingdom and his proclamation of the will of God, Bultmann implies that before he was an eschatologist, Jesus was an existentialist: the real issue was the achievement of the true self, but Jesus happened to express himself in the language of contemporary ("primitive") Jewish beliefs. It is extremely improbable, however, that Jesus had any notion of achieving one's true self through decision, even in "primitive" form (whatever that may mean); more likely, he actually believed that the time of judgment was near. Jesus undoubtedly was an existentialist to the extent that he was concerned with the situation of man before God and other men, but it is not apparent that he had any idea of human existence as a recurrent crisis of decision, or of man's achieving his true self prior to or apart from his certainty that God was about to bring his Kingdom. Instead of saying that Jesus was an existentialist who clothed his real understanding of human existence in the mythological garments of eschatology, it would be more accurate to say that in his eschatological message, Jesus expressed a definite understanding of human existence: that man is responsible before God for what he does in his life; that God judges or will judge him, but is gracious and will be gracious to those who turn to him. Such an understanding of human existence *may* certainly be expressed in Bultmann's existentialist categories, but it is not correct, nor is it necessary, to attribute these categories to Jesus in order to indicate the meaning of Jesus' understanding of human existence.

Bultmann exaggerates the difference between his own interpretation and the interim ethics theory. Actually, there is little difference between "repentance" or "moral renewal" as understood by Schweitzer, and "decision" or "radical obedience" as Bultmann understands these terms. In either case, the response is to be translated into action in the concrete situations of life in this interim or now before the coming of the Kingdom. In both cases, obedience to Jesus' proclamation of God's will is the condition of admission into the Kingdom. Schweitzer maintained that Jesus' ethic is relevant to modern man despite the facts that the Kingdom did not come and that Jesus did not intend his teaching/preaching for future generations. What is Bultmann's position with respect to the *contemporary* significance of Jesus and his message?

The Significance of Jesus and His Message

The Jesus of History and the Christ of the Kerygma

It was obvious to Bultmann, as it had been to Schweitzer, that the historical Jesus is to our time a stranger and an enigma. The authority of the historical Jesus is limited to his own time. But the Christ of the kerygma is not so confined. It is the latter that bridges the gap of time and *Weltanschauungen* between the former and our own era.

> Do the authoritative claims of Jesus, perceived as a historical phenomenon, extend beyond the time of his earthly activity? Does the claim and promise of the historical Jesus in his "immediacy" extend to later generations? This is precisely what occurs in the kerygma, in which it is not the historical Jesus, but rather the risen Lord who says, "All authority has been given to me." The Christ of the kerygma has, as it were, displaced the historical Jesus and authoritatively addresses the hearer—every hearer.[101]

That being the case, the question naturally occurs, What is the relationship between the historical Jesus and the Christ of the kerygma? just as with Schweitzer, the question appeared as to the relationship, if any, between the "Spirit" or "person" of

Jesus and the Jesus of history. Precisely this question has been at the center of the discussions and controversies among the so-called "post-Bultmannian" proponents of the "new quest of the historical Jesus," and also, to some extent, between them and Bultmann himself. In fact, the rather ungracious term "post-Bultmannian" refers primarily to the claim put forth by some of Bultmann's former pupils that they have moved beyond the apparent dichotomy in Bultmann's position between the historical Jesus and the Christ of the kerygma. Bultmann, as is well known, finds that Jesus thought of himself as no more than the prophetic and eschatological messenger of the last times. He spoke of the imminent coming of the Kingdom of God and of the Son of Man, who was probably someone other than himself. He did not regard himself either as the Messiah or as one who would come as Messiah; nor did he predict his death or see in it any eschatological or saving significance. In short, Jesus remained a Jew; he was not a Christian, though his life and death are presupposed in the preaching (kerygma) of the early church. The kerygma, on the other hand, proclaimed Jesus Christ, the crucified and risen Lord and Messiah, who had ascended to heaven, who would come on the clouds of heaven as Messiah or Son of Man, who had already become God's "eschatological act of salvation."[102]

The proponents of the "old quest" wished to resolve the discrepancy between the historical Jesus and the Christ of the church's preaching in favor of the former: the latter was to be eliminated or reduced to the significance of husk. The proponents of the "new quest" wish to narrow the gap between the historical Jesus and the kerygmatic Christ by interpreting the former in terms of the latter. They attempt to show, for instance, some correspondence between Jesus' understanding of existence and that presented or mediated in the church's preaching, that Jesus himself believed that the Kingdom of God was in some sense already present during his lifetime, and that he knew himself to be the Messiah. It is still too early to determine how successful these efforts have been.[103]

It is interesting that Bultmann himself evidently intends

the kerygma as a line of continuity between the historical Jesus and ourselves. Not only was Jesus the presupposition of the church's preaching, but his preaching was also "taken up in" the church's preaching.[104] In his essay, "Jesus and Paul," Bultmann points to a whole series of similarities between the preaching of Jesus and that of Paul. But the basic connection between the modern believer and the historical Jesus is in the repetition of "the eschatological event that has its origin in Jesus" through the preaching of the contemporary church:

> This eschatological event is, in its paradoxical identity with the historical event, never a bygone event, but it is fulfilled again and again in the preaching of the Church.[105]

By "eschatological event," Bultmann means the preaching of the church's message, which presents the hearer with the possibility of a new understanding of existence based on the Christ event. Thus, the kerygma itself, in Bultmann's terms, is an "eschatological event." Instead of the "timeless" gospel or words of Jesus, Bultmann has, in its place, a timeless, or recurrent "kerygma" (or eschatological event) which addresses "every hearer."[106] This kerygma "has put itself in the place of the historical Jesus; it represents him."[107] Bultmann even goes on to say that "Jesus is really present in the kerygma, that it is *his* word which involves the hearer in the kerygma."[108] And yet Bultmann insists, especially against J. M. Robinson, that the church's message about the Christ totally disregards any repetition of the teaching or proclamation of Jesus.[109] One can only conclude that Bultmann's position with respect to the relationship between the historical Jesus and the kerygma remains unclear. He would like to maintain that Jesus and his word or message are present to the believer, but he is afraid that if the kerygma could be shown to correspond with Jesus' own understanding of his identity and purpose, the former would be "legitimated" by the findings of historical research with respect to the latter, and the result would be a false security in place of the Lutheran (or Kierkegaardian) leap of faith.[110] Cahill feels that Bultmann's fear about "substituting research for faith" arises out of his "radical Lutheran orientation."[111] In any case, this fear is mistaken and irrelevant. It is mistaken because historical research cannot demonstrate the truthfulness of religious belief, e.g., that Jesus really was the Messiah; it can show only, within limits of the evidence and probability, that the early Christians, or Jesus himself, believed him to be that figure. It is irrelevant in the same way that any religious belief is irrelevant in dealing with a historical question. Whether the historian believes that Jesus was the Christ or not, he should be free to draw such conclusions as are indicated in the evidence. Confusion with respect to the latter point is evident in Harvey and Ogden's critique of Robinson, where they grant that "historical research could never establish that Jesus' demand is the action of God," but then express concern lest historical research might (on Robinson's approach) undercut or "disconfirm" the kerygma if it should turn out that Jesus' self-understanding was *not* the same as that which the kerygma attributed to him. In such a case, anxiety would arise "because faith is made dependent on the results of historical criticism."[112] Such a consideration, of course, is no argument against Robinson's position, since historical research could not prove the ultimate truth or falsity of either "self-understanding," and the historian should not be deterred from finding such a discrepancy by fear of discovering any theological difficulties. The decisive point against Robinson's position is not that it might produce anxiety among the faithful, but that it is historically untenable: the kerygma does not, as Robinson claims, proclaim "Jesus' own existential selfhood."[113]

Harnack wished to scrape away all accretions—both Jewish nationalistic and eschatological and Christian ritual and dogmatic—in order to arrive at a permanently valid gospel. Bultmann wishes to demythologize the ancient eschatology and world view in order to arrive at a permanently valid kerygma. Significantly, Bultmann does not differentiate between dogma and kerygma. Just as Harnack experienced considerable difficulty in arriving at a single (or even triple) definition of "the

Gospel," so also Bultmann produces a variety of summaries of the content of the kerygma. For instance, he writes, "In the kerygma Jesus Christ is proclaimed as the one who died vicariously on the cross for the sins of men and was miraculously raised by God for our salvation."[114] This phraseology seems more influenced by later Christian creeds than by early Christian preaching. Two pages later, he asserts that "the kerygma maintains that God has made the historical Jesus the Christ, the *Kyrios* (Acts 2:36)," and "contains the paradoxical assertion that a historical event—the historical Jesus and his history—is the eschatological event (the end of the age and what it implies)."[115] In this last statement, it is apparent that Bultmann is putting his own interpretation into the mouth of the kerygma, in the same way that liberal writers ascribed their interpretations to Jesus. One could extend the list of Bultmann's summaries of the substance of the kerygma indefinitely. Occasionally he uses other phrases in the same sense as kerygma: "the gospel," "the New Testament," and "Christian faith."[116] It is not clear how he would define these concepts with respect to one another; he seems to use them synonymously. Furthermore, he often hypostatizes these terms, especially "the New Testament" and "the kerygma," as if the New Testament could "understand human existence" or "say" something on that (or any other) subject; or as if the kerygma might or might not "be interested" in something, for example, history, or presuppose, claim, or intend various things.[117] This is the language of myth. If one were a Catholic, one might even speculate whether Bultmann or the post-Bultmannians may eventually attempt to elevate the kerygma to the status of an hypostasis of the Trinity. Evidently, Bultmann is serious when he states that the church's kerygma has replaced the historical Jesus. But, as Robinson has pointed out, Bultmann uses the term "kerygma" in two different senses: one is the church's act of preaching, the other is the content of that preaching.[118] Whatever the relation between the historical Jesus and the content of the church's preaching, the *act* of preaching does not—sacramentally or otherwise—reproduce the "Christ event" or "eschatological event," despite Bultmann's claim that the kerygma "represents the historical Jesus," or that "Jesus is really present in the kerygma."[119] Despite his evident desire that it were otherwise (in spite of his Lutheran qualms about legitimizing the faith), Bultmann is unable to bridge the gap between the historical Jesus and his message, on the one hand, and the Christ who is significant for faith on the other. But the case is quite different with respect to Bultmann's understanding of the significance of the historical Jesus and his message for the *moral life* of modern man.

Jesus' Significance for Ethics

The late H. Richard Niebuhr used to state that in his judgment, one of Bultmann's major concerns was ethics. Curiously, there is little evidence of interest in this aspect of Bultmann's thought on the part of the so-called "post-Bultmannians." Their attention seems engaged mainly in the so-called "new quest," "new hermeneutics," and "new historiography." Even Bultmann himself has made no effort to develop a theory of ethics. Perhaps this lack of interest is consistent with his understanding of the nature of moral decision: in the existential vacuum, one will know what to do without reference to theories or norms. Nevertheless, in Bultmann's writings one finds evidence of a fairly unified conception of ethics.

Although Bultmann nowhere discusses the significance of Jesus and his message for ethics as a separate problem or topic, it is evident that *Bultmann conceives of ethics primarily as response to the message of Jesus.* Because of the problematic character of Bultmann's understanding of the relation between the historical Jesus and the kerygma, this fact has generally escaped notice. Possibly Bultmann himself is unaware of it. Perhaps it is because of his feeling that Jesus' message is fundamentally relevant to the moral life of the modern Christian that Bultmann continues to find a place for the word of Jesus in the kerygma, despite his insistence that the kerygma has to do only with the "that," but not the "what" or "how," of the historical Jesus.[120] In any case, Bultmann presents Jesus and his "word" or message as the basis for the Christian moral life.

The direct authority and validity of Jesus' words is indicated in numerous places where Bultmann writes of their meaning for us. Such statements appear regularly in his volume of *Marburg Sermons,* nearly half of which are on Synoptic texts. Jesus exhorts "us" to "consider the lilies of the field" and not to be anxious. There is much acute need in the world, yet "these words of the Master" are an admonition that one should do all that one can "to ensure that such words can be suitably addressed to all mankind."[121]

> Jesus . . . enjoins us to seek first the Kingdom of God and His righteousness. Our lives must be controlled by the concern for God's Kingdom. The sovereignty of God and the will of God must be placed first in our lives.[122]

Preaching on Luke 18:9–14 he says, "If we do not feel that we are perhaps intended by Jesus' reference to the Pharisee, then it is to be feared that we have not rightly understood it, and listened to it."[123] And, on Luke 14:16–24:

> But if Jesus is speaking to us to-day through this parable, then He is summoning us also to consider whether we do not belong to the category of the original guests, who have long accepted God's call . . . but who, when the matter becomes serious, calling for decision in the present moment, prefer to be absorbed in private affairs and to despise God's summons.[124]

In the same sermon, he points to the meaning for us of Jesus' words at the great judgment (Matt. 25:42 f., 45):

> Just as at the time of Jesus it was His appearance itself which embodied God's call . . . so since those days, His call has sounded everywhere and time and time again, as Jesus Himself confronts us everywhere and time and time again. Where does He meet us? Where have we failed to perceive His presence or to hear His call? Jesus Himself has anticipated this question. To those who have failed to apprehend His presence in life, the following words apply: "I was hungry and you gave me no food. . . ."[125]

Perhaps these examples will suffice by way of showing that in Bultmann's judgment, Jesus and his words have the utmost significance for us today, at least with respect to our moral stance before God and our neighbor.[126] But, it might be objected, this is only the way Bultmann talks in his *sermons.* After all, historians and even (or especially) theologians "have always been able to abandon their academic tools while ascending to the pulpit."[127] But Bultmann says the same thing in his scholarly works as well. For example, in *Primitive Christianity,* he makes clear his understanding that Jesus' commandment of love (Mark 12:28–34) and the parable of the good Samaritan apply to *us:*

> And what does God really require? Love. . . . The parable of the Good Samaritan shows that there is no difficulty in seeing what we ought to do when our neighbour needs our help. . . . We all know how we would like others to treat us if we were in the same situation ourselves. . . . His demand is always present anew in each successive encounter with our neighbour.[128]

In *Jesus Christ and Mythology,* he undertakes to demythologize and interpret the meaning of *Jesus'* eschatological preaching "for modern man," for "us."[129]

Bultmann comes closest to developing a programmatic statement with respect to the character and significance of Jesus' "ethics" in *Jesus and the Word.* It is important, first of all, to reiterate that for Bultmann, the historical Jesus, who with his "word," i.e., message, was the subject of that study, has no place in the kerygma or New Testament theology other than as presupposition: "The Jesus of history is not kerygma, any more than my book [*Jesus and the Word*] was."[130] And yet in that very book, Bultmann undertook to set forth the validity of Jesus and his word for us! In his introduction to this book, he says that in it, "attention is entirely limited to what he [Jesus] *purposed,* and hence to what in his purpose as a part of history makes a present demand on us."[131] What Jesus purposed, he finds, was that men should be radically obedient to the will of God. Bultmann's purpose in this book, clearly, is not merely to describe Jesus' message, but to indicate its consequence for the moral life of men today: "The investigation really concerns the content, meaning, and *validity for us* of what is taught in the gospels."[132]

It has generally been overlooked that Bultmann develops his theory of the ethics of radical obedience *as an interpretation of Jesus' teaching* concerning what God requires of man. *The ethics of radical obedience is the ethics of Jesus.* Radical obedience does not mean, to Bultmann, simply a higher (or more subservient) form of obedience to God's authority. It means the perception and acceptance of that which is to be done as something which one desires to do, in one's free, willing, and glad response to God's command and to the neighbor's need: "Radical obedience exists only when a man inwardly assents to what is required of him, when the thing commanded is seen as intrinsically God's command."[133] Bultmann insists that radical obedience involves the renunciation of one's own will in the presence of God, and love in the presence of the neighbor: "As I can love my neighbor only when I surrender my will completely to God's will, so I can love God only while I will what He wills, while I really love my neighbor."[134] The love commandment is the essential substance of Jesus' proclamation of God's will, of radical obedience, and, therefore, also the basis for Christian ethics. Bultmann's description of "the Christian commandment of neighbor love"[135] *exactly parallels* his conception of Jesus' "commandment of love" described in *Jesus and the Word.*

The Christian ethic, he says, is an "ethic of obligation" or "obedience."[136] This obedience finds expression in the "Christian command of neighbor-love."[137] Christian love, like Jesus' idea of love, consists in renouncing one's own claim, and living *for* the neighbor, being responsive to the need of the neighbor as one encounters him:

> It [love] requires overcoming of self and serving the other in the concrete situation of life in which he encounters me.

> Jesus thought of love . . . as an overcoming of self-will in the concrete situation of life in which a man encounters other men.[138]

The Christian commandment of neighbor-love does not say *what* I must do; what one is to do is sufficiently indicated by the words "as thyself" or the "Golden Rule":

> *What* the man is to do is sufficiently said through the reference to natural self-love. Since he loves himself, he knows how he wants to be loved by others; if he would love others, he will also know what he must do for them.[139]

> What am I then to do . . . ? . . . Self-love is not a principle of morality, but the attitude of the natural man. If a man then is to love his neighbor as himself, he knows very well how to direct his conduct in the concrete situation.[140]

There is no standard theory of ethics to which one may have recourse. The Christian is expected to know in the concrete situation of encounter with the neighbor what to do:

> The love command trusts man and expects that in the concrete situation of the life of his neighbor, he will see and know what he has to do. There is, therefore, no Christian ethic in the sense of an intelligible theory concerning what the Christian must do or refrain from doing.[141]

> *Jesus teaches no ethics at all* in the sense of an intelligible theory valid for all men concerning what should be done and left undone. . . . [Jesus] can only leave the decision to the man in his concrete situation. If a man really loves, he knows already what he has to do.[142]

Bultmann's understanding of *Christian* ethics is indistinguishable from his interpretation of the kind of ethical response demanded by Jesus: obedience to the commandment to love the neighbor, guided by the neighbor's need in the concrete situation and the words "as thyself," but with no other "standard." Perhaps the point need no longer be belabored: *Bultmann's conception of Christian ethics is coincident with, and based upon his understanding of, the meaning of Jesus' teaching, particularly, the demand for radical obedience.*

If this thesis is correct, a whole series of new questions appears in connection with Bultmann's theological position. Why does Bultmann look only to the kerygma for Christian faith and doctrine, but turn to the historical Jesus and his message for Christian ethics? What, if any, is the significance of the New Testament, specifically the Pauline and Johannine, ethic of the "indicative-imperative," "eschatological existence," or "grace and freedom"[143] for the modern Christian? What is the relationship between the decision called for in the church's preaching ("freedom for the future," "the possibility of a new self-understanding") and that in response to the demand of Jesus (for "radical obedience")? What, in short, is Bultmann's conception of the relation between faith and ethics? Bultmann himself has recently noted the distinction, but without defining the relationship: "This demand of faith (which is at the same time a gift) does not spring out of the ethical situation and should not be confused with obedience to the ethical demand."[144] Perhaps answers to these questions will become clearer in future Bultmann research.

Certain sources of confusion or difficulty in Bultmann's conception of ethics have already been indicated. For one thing, the concept "radical obedience" is misleading. What Bultmann really seems to mean is radical *love*. Undoubtedly, Bultmann is correct in seeing this in terms of the Hebraic-Jewish-Christian conception of ethics as obedience to God, rather than as some kind of virtue, value, or ideal.[145] But Bultmann tends to obscure the nature of love when he defines it as "simply the requirement of obedience," or only negatively, as "the overcoming of the self," "the surrender of one's own claim," or only formally, as "an attitude of the will."[146] These definitions abstract the self from what H. Richard Niebuhr aptly designated the triadic relationship with God and neighbor. Love is not simply the overcoming of the self, an ascetic exercise, but, as Bultmann himself *sometimes* says, it consists in serving the other.[147] Love certainly is not simply "obedience"; obedience becomes love only when one relates oneself positively and helpfully to one's neighbor. Love is "an attitude of the will," but more specifically, it is the affirmation of the well-being of one's neighbor, the will or desire to do what is good for him. *Love of neighbor,* active concern for his well-being, *is,* in fact, *the substance of radical obedience.*

This point, which Bultmann often makes quite clearly, is, nevertheless, also obscured frequently by his restriction of interest to the individual in his existential decision for his own future. As long as attention is focused on the individual, achieving his own "true self" or "existence" through his "decision,"[148] the neighbor is at most a secondary concern, and may even drop out of view altogether, as in the case of Harnack's individualistic epitome of the Kingdom of God, "God and the soul, the soul and its God," where there is no mention of the neighbor or his "soul." What Bultmann really means, but does not always bring to clarity, is that the new self-understanding of faith frees one from selfishness, for love of neighbor.

A related problem appears in connection with Bultmann's conception of moral decision as something that takes place in an existential vacuum. In the crisis of decision, Bultmann supposes, "man knows what is *now* good and evil . . . not on the basis of any past experience or rational deductions, but directly from the immediate situation."[149] Bultmann's point is well taken: one cannot responsibly fall back on a code of law or a textbook on ethics when moral decisions are to be made. One must attempt to determine in each situation what is happening, and how the well-being of the various persons involved is being affected. But this is exactly the point that Bultmann fails to bring into focus. In the concrete situation, one does not automatically "know what is *now* good and evil." One does, however, have a "standard" or point of reference: what is *good for* the neighbor or neighbors involved in the situation. In order to know this, one must not only examine the facts of the "situation" (which often are not how they appear on the surface or at first glance), and make "rational deductions" about them, but also use as much of one's "past experience" with respect to similar situations and, particularly, with respect to what is truly good for or harmful to persons. It is even possible that some of the "laws," "values," and "ideals" of the community may embody the wisdom of past experience with respect to what is helpful or harmful to persons, even if these are not to be sought as absolutes or refuges from responsibility. One must also, if possible, take into account the past experience of the persons involved, as well as their hopes and expectations for the future. One can hardly imagine any social or political question of consequence where such considerations could be neglected without harmful consequences.

Bultmann's description of the nature of moral decision in "the moment" is further confused because he refuses to recognize as legitimate the ambiguities that arise out of conflicting claims and values. Instead, he is under the illusion that in every situation, there is one and only one valid solution or response:

> Obedience will always take place as *decision* between concrete possibilities. However, decision means the choice to hear *one* command as the divine requirement out of the multitude of voices of concrete commands.[150]

Here responsibility gives way to a mysticism of the moment.

One final point about Bultmann's conception of ethics: its relevance to man's life in society and history. Bultmann has been accused of indifference to "real man in real history," who is not only an isolated individual, confronting a series of isolated neighbors in discrete (and unique) crises of decision, but "is also the member of institutions" where such proximate norms as equal justice and international order must be achieved in the face of complicated conditions and conflicting claims.[151] Bultmann concedes that he never "participated in political affairs."[152] Bultmann expressed his opposition to Hitler only tacitly, through the Confessing Church, and throughout World War II evinced concern and gratitude for "our fighting men" (i.e., the German armies).[153] After the war, however, he disclosed a critical awareness of what had happened in and to his nation as a result of its acceptance of the ideal of "will to self-assertion and power springing from the race."[154] He had lost a brother in each of the world wars. Neither Harnack nor Bultmann developed a social ethic. Both were aware that Jesus had presented no "social program." But like Harnack, Bultmann perceived that Christians are not thereby exempt from the need to concern themselves with "the social distresses of our time," and that "in practice," Jesus' commandment of love "may have far-reaching implications for national and social life in general."[155]

Bultmann devoted his attention primarily to the nature of moral decision, the personal or existential response of obedience to God and of love to neighbor in the concrete situation of individual, person-to-person encounter. It is here that he made his greatest contribution to ethics, both in describing Jesus' teaching of radical obedience and in suggesting how this teaching may be valid for us. He should not be judged severely because he did not also, like Reinhold Niebuhr, attempt to present a thoroughgoing critique of the moral life of man in historical, political, and economic societies. There are, after all, many helpful gifts. Bultmann makes it clear, however, that he is aware of the importance of this undertaking. Unlike Schweitzer, he was not temperamentally or by conviction opposed to institutional reform:

> Certainly the Christian, as one who believes and loves, has the obligation to seek means by which social existence may gain a form in which genuine human personal life is possible. He is, therefore, also responsible for institutions in which a life of freedom and responsibility is possible, and for the ordering of social existence through justice and righteousness.[156]

Bultmann correctly perceives that the Christian cannot escape from responsibility toward his neighbors in society with the excuse that Jesus did not interest himself in social questions such as justice. The fact that Jesus did not lay down a social program gives to each man the burden and freedom to decide what radical love requires of him in the presence of his neighbor and community. As Harnack put it, Jesus' command of love is "profoundly socialistic." When the well-being of one's neighbors is at stake, radical obedient love cannot ignore their needs. In the "Sermon on the Mount," Bultmann finds:

> The idea is also implied—though without being explicitly stated—that justice has a legitimate meaning when it stands in the service of the demand of love, or, in practical terms, when it serves the community. This implication was clearly seen by Luther. Moreover, with the idea that justice receives its meaning from the demand of love there is also given a criterion for criticizing and further developing positive justice; and this is true however little Jesus himself was interested in any such further development of it.[157]

Reinhold Niebuhr might have written as much. Bultmann's conception of ethics, and thus also his understanding of the significance of Jesus and his message for the moral life, has been overlooked for the most part in recent studies of ethics and Bultmann research. One can expect that the future will bring a greater appreciation of the importance of these aspects of his work.

CHAPTER IV

Recent British and American Interpretations

CHARLES HAROLD DODD (1884–): THE ETHICS OF REALIZED ESCHATOLOGY

C. H. Dodd, together with most other British scholars, rejects the assumption of form critics that the earliest tradition of Jesus' life and teaching existed wholly in the form of independent units which were later artificially or arbitrarily put together by the Evangelists.[1] At some points, he concedes, the Marcan chronology has been interrupted by topical groupings, and the precise sequence may not always be correct in every detail. "Yet there is good reason to believe that in broad outlines the Marcan order does represent a genuine succession of events, within which movement and development can be traced."[2] Dodd believes that the narrative summaries in Mark present a more or less accurate historical and chronological outline which corresponds to and is verified by the accounts of Jesus' activity in the primitive kerygma of the church.[3] Like many British writers, Dodd follows B. H. Streeter's "four-source" theory, and finds Mark and Q reliable sources for Jesus' ministry and teaching.[4] He rejects the idea (which he attributes to Bultmann) that nearly all the ethical teaching imputed to Jesus originated in the early church as "an exaggerated reaction from the 'liberal' view of Jesus as a moral teacher and nothing more."[5]

The Life of Jesus

Dodd finds Jesus' ministry divided into two periods: a period "when the outstanding feature of the situation was the obduracy of the people of Galilee,"[6] and a period dominated by the movement toward Jerusalem and his passion. Dodd offers little explanation for the transition from the one period to the other:

> *Galilee has grown too hot to hold him.* In his retirement he is enlisting volunteers for a dangerous enterprise. He leads them up to Jerusalem, rides into the city with a crowd at his back, clears the temple of the money changers who do business in its courts, and challenges the ecclesiastical authorities on their own ground.[7]

Dodd does not indicate what, if anything, he thinks Jesus meant to accomplish by this procedure. Evidently it had nothing to do with the coming of the Kingdom of God, nor with Jesus' disclosure as the Messiah, for—in Dodd's theory—the Kingdom had already come, and Jesus lived as Messiah throughout his public ministry.

Dodd nowhere discusses the problem of the Messianic secret, a fact that is surprising considering the confidence he places in the Marcan tradition where that "secret" is embedded. Dodd has no doubt that Jesus regarded himself as the Messiah: the one who *had* come, and who in coming *had* brought the Kingdom of God. His coming and the coming of the Kingdom presented men with a crisis, a time of decision: he called upon men to receive the Kingdom which was fully realized in his own ministry. Dodd is not sure whether Jesus went to Jerusalem in order "to make a last appeal" or "to offer Himself to death." In either case, his Messianic career could "find its fitting climax" only in Jerusalem; in going to Jerusalem, he was setting the stage for "the predestined Messianic conflict in which the Kingdom of God should be revealed."[8] Jesus regarded his death as a self-sacrifice for the many, which was necessary "to bring about a new order of relations between God and man, a new covenant."[9]

This interpretation seems to resemble Schweitzer's: Jesus went to Jerusalem intending to bear the Messianic woes in lieu of the suffering of "many," and thereby bring about the appearance of the final age. Dodd, however, does not attempt to explain the connection between Jesus' activities in Jerusalem and the forthcoming eschatological events. Moreover, Dodd maintains elsewhere that the Kingdom of God had already fully appeared in Jesus' ministry. It is not clear, then, how Jesus could bring about such a "new order" by going to Jerusalem.

The Kingdom of God: Realized Eschatology

According to Dodd, as Jesus understood it, the Kingdom of God was not going to come in the future; it was already here. In fact, Jesus did not understand the Kingdom of God as an event or era: it is "an order beyond space and time."[10] The Kingdom became actualized in time and space, however, in Jesus' ministry, Dodd claims. Bultmann suggested, somewhat ambiguously, that the early church believed something of the sort; Dodd states that such was Jesus' own understanding as well:

> Jesus declares that this ultimate, the Kingdom of God, has come into history, and He takes upon Himself the "eschatological" role of the "Son of Man." The absolute, the "wholly other," has entered into time and space. And as the Kingdom of God has come and the Son of Man has come, so also judgment and blessedness have come into human experience.[11]

Dodd sees all the eschatological events present in Jesus' ministry: the appearance (Parousia) of the Messiah, the coming of the Kingdom, and the time of judgment. He does admit, however, that "there remains a residue of eschatology which is not exhausted in the 'realized eschatology' of the Gospel, namely, the element of sheer finality." Whatever this "element of sheer finality" may mean for Dodd, it is not related, evidently, to the Parousia and judgment.[12] Not only does Dodd claim that Jesus regarded the judgment as present; he also, in effect, rendered the Judge superfluous: men pass judgment upon themselves, as they respond with repentance or indifference to Jesus' appeal.[13] Here Dodd's interpretation may be influenced, as elsewhere, by his reliance upon the Fourth Gospel. Dodd apparently does not consider it necessary to "demythologize," for Jesus himself—at any rate, the Johannine Jesus—has already obligingly fulfilled and translated the eschatological myths into ultimate realities which men of any and all times henceforth can experience.

The passage that Dodd cites most frequently as evidence for realized eschatology is Matt. 12:28 (= Luke 11:20), where the verb *phthanein* ("to arrive") appears instead of the usual *engizein* ("to come near"). Here, in Jesus' exorcism of demons, Dodd says, it is evident that the power of God is at work in the world, a fact that can only mean that "the 'eschatological' Kingdom of God is proclaimed as a present fact."[14] Dodd thinks that the same meaning was intended in Mark 1:14 f. and in Luke 10:9–11 where the verb *engizein* is used. He grants that "on the face of it" *engizein* might mean that the Kingdom of God is only "near"; but urges that in the Septuagint, the two Semitic roots *naga'* and *meta',* meaning "to reach" or "arrive" are translated by both *phthanein* and *engizein,* and that both Greek verbs therefore mean that the Kingdom of God has arrived.[15] He accounts for the fact that John would have announced that the Kingdom of God had come (*engizein*) prior to the beginning of Jesus' ministry (Matt. 3:2) by declaring that Matthew "has here mistakenly attributed words of Jesus to the Baptist."[16]

Dodd finds the "plain meaning" of Luke 16:16 (= Matt. 11:12 f.), "the most explicit [passages] of their kind," to be that Jesus thought the Kingdom not imminent, but "here." "John the Baptist marks the dividing line: before him, the law and the prophets; after him, the Kingdom of God. Any interim period is excluded."[17] In his Preface to the third edition of *The Parables,* however, Dodd acknowledges that "the passage is a notorious *crux interpretum,* and I am not at all sure that I understand it." He also grants that possibly, as Matthew viewed it,

> there *was* an "interim period" between the baptism of John and the coming of the Kingdom of God, the period, namely, of our Lord's earthly ministry. Yet even for him the Kingdom of God must have been in some sense a present reality . . . , since it is said to be the object of human "force" (whatever that may mean).[18]

Dodd's admission that he does not know what the passage may mean does not, evidently, weaken his certainty that it supports realized eschatology!

Dodd also claims to find support for realized eschatology elsewhere in the Synoptic Gospels,[19] but places his greatest reliance on the passages just noted. Dodd feels that they are sufficient to establish his case: "The sayings which declare the Kingdom of God to have come are *explicit* and *unequivocal.* They are moreover the most *characteristic* and *distinctive* of the Gospel sayings on the subject."[20] In view of the qualifications that have been mentioned, it is apparent that Dodd has exaggerated the certainty of his interpretation of these passages. That interpretation may be possible, but the meaning of these passages is scarcely "explicit and unequivocal," and they are certainly not "characteristic and distinctive."

Dodd's Treatment of the Futuristic Evidence

Dodd is willing to admit, if indirectly, that there are passages that show that Jesus believed that the Kingdom would come as a future event. For instance, he says:

> If we look at the reported sayings of Jesus, we shall find that alongside sayings which point to the future consummation there are sayings, at least equally plain and striking, which speak of the epoch-making significance of the present.[21]

How does he propose to reconcile these two kinds of sayings? Schweitzer had regarded all the sayings as dominated, whether explicitly or not, by the eschatological outlook; Wrede had attributed the eschatological sayings to the church, a theory designated by Schweitzer as the "literary solution" to the problem of eschatology. Dodd proposes to reject both the "eschatological" and the "literary" solutions.

With respect to the former, he concedes, reluctantly, that "it does appear that Jesus spoke in terms of current apocalypse of a 'divine event,' in which He would Himself appear in glory as Son of Man."

> If then these "apocalyptic" predictions are to be understood literally, they seem to point to an event expected to happen very soon indeed, and this is the view commonly taken by those who adopt the "eschatological" interpretation of the Gospels. But, as they clearly see, this raises a difficulty in regard to the ethical teaching of Jesus. Some of them have attempted to represent this ethical teaching as "interim ethics," in the sense of precepts for the life of the disciples during the very short interval before normal conditions of human life cease to be. But it has become clear that the sayings cannot be convincingly interpreted in this sense.[22]

Dodd does not explain why he is unconvinced by the interim ethics interpretation. The fact that an interpretation may present a theological "difficulty" is no argument against its historical accuracy. As will become evident, Dodd's treatment of the eschatological interpretation, and thus also of interim ethics, does less than justice to these theories and the evidence they account for. Here Dodd reveals what will be apparent elsewhere, that his theory of realized eschatology arises out of certain dogmatic or philosophical interests. Dodd admits the possibility of an "interim period" coincident with Jesus' ministry and prior to the arrival of the Kingdom, but insists, nevertheless, that "any interim period is excluded."[23] Why it is excluded is not apparent. He attempts to explain away Schweitzer's theory of "consistent eschatology" as a "compromise":

> In the presence of one set of sayings which appeared to contemplate the coming of the Kingdom of God as future, and another set which appeared to contemplate it as already present, they offered an interpretation which represented it as coming very, very soon.[24]

This "explanation" of the origin of the eschatological interpretation is simply untrue, and fails to account for such Synoptic evidence as Luke 12:58 f., which, Dodd admits, refers to the critical situation of Jesus' hearers, who have only "a few moments" in which to act;[25] or Matt. 10:23; or Matt. 10:7 = Luke 10:9; 10:11; and Mark 1:15, where the verb *engizein* ("to come near") is found. However Dodd may interpret these verses, they were not invented by Schweitzer! Dodd's interpretation of Mark 9:1 is necessarily strained: "The meaning appears to be that some of those who heard Jesus speak would before their death awake to the fact that the Kingdom of God had come."[26]

The literary solution, Dodd *says*,[27] is not acceptable either:

> We seem to be confronted with two diverse strains in the teaching of Jesus, one of which appears to contemplate the indefinite continuance of human life under historical conditions, while the other appears to suggest a speedy end to these conditions. A drastic criticism might eliminate the one strain or the other, but both are deeply embedded in the earliest form of tradition known to us. It would be better to admit that we do not possess the key to their reconciliation than to do such violence to our documents.[28]

It might be expected that he would conclude that the problem is unanswerable, or that its answer is to be sought in a paradox. But Dodd believes that he has the key after all. He continues: "It may be possible to find a place for both strains if we make full allowance for the symbolic character of the 'apocalyptic' sayings."[29]

The "Symbolic" Solution

In an earlier book, before he had developed the realized eschatology theory, Dodd had declared that even if Jesus sometimes "used" apocalyptic "imagery," he had not taken such images seriously: "He never identified the Kingdom of God with any of these dreams."[30] Instead, Dodd urged, for Jesus, "the Kingdom of God means God reigning, reigning in the hearts of men, and reigning in the whole sphere of their outward life as well, individual and corporate."[31] Like the liberals of Harnack's era, Dodd sometimes treats the Kingdom of God as a phenomenon of religious experience: "The coming of the Kingdom of God is realized in experience."[32] In any case, Dodd maintains that Jesus' eschatological language is to be taken as symbolic of spiritual and timeless, rather than tangible and future, realities:

> The imagery therefore retains its significance as symbolizing the eternal realities, which though they enter into history are never exhausted in it. The Son of Man has come, but also He will come; the sin of men is judged, but also it will be judged.
>
> But these future tenses are only an accommodation of language. There is no coming of the Son of Man "after" His coming in Galilee and Jerusalem, whether soon or late, for there is no before and after in the eternal order. . . . That which cannot be experienced in history is symbolized by the picture of a coming event, and its timeless quality is expressed as pure simultaneity in time—"as the lightning flashes."[33]

In his more recent books, Dodd no longer proposes that Jesus meant to symbolize "the rule of God in men's hearts" by his use of apocalyptic language; rather, he had in mind "the eternal order," which was "beyond space and time."[34] Dodd moved from a liberal to a Platonic interpretation of the meaning of the Kingdom.

In Jesus' ministry, life, and death, this "eternal order" was manifested in time, an event of decisive significance for his contemporaries and for all men since.[35] In this manifestation of the eternal order, "the eternal *issues* are laid bare," "the eternal *significance of history* had revealed itself."[36] One must ask, however, whether it is plausible, as Dodd assumes, that Jesus really had in mind "the eternal issues" or "the eternal significance of history" but spoke instead of "the Kingdom of God" in order to symbolize these realities. Why did he veil his real meaning by using this "symbolic" language?

This revelation of "the eternal issues" or "the eternal significance of history," Dodd continues, called men to decision; it precipitated a "brief and tremendous crisis" in human existence. The parables of the "Unjust Steward" (Luke 16:1–7) and the "Defendant" (Luke 12:57 ff.) refer to "the urgency of taking the right step in face of the tremendous crisis" in which men "must act, now or never."[37] It is not clear, however, in Dodd's interpretation, why it will soon be too late for men to act. What is about to happen that occasions this urgency by limiting the possibility of action beyond the immediate future? Dodd rules out the view that Jesus expected the Kingdom momentarily and therefore called on men to respond in the critical interim before its appearance. But how does realized eschatology explain the urgency of the situation confronting Jesus' hearers?

The Political-Historical and Literary Solutions

Dodd offers an ingenious interpretation of the parables of the "Faithful and Unfaithful Servants" (Matt. 24:45–51 = Luke 12:42–46), the "Waiting Servants" (Luke 12:35–38 = Mark 13:33–37), and the "Ten Virgins" (Matt. 25:1–12). All these seemingly eschatological parables actually referred to unexpected *political* or *historical* crises, such as the authorities' attack on Jesus and his disciples, for which they must be ready at all times, or the impending destruction of the Temple and the Jewish nation by the Romans.[38] The eschatological aspect of these parables, Dodd urges, was subsequently added by the early church. His interpretation of these three parables seems particularly forced. These parables may well reflect the need of the church to explain the delay in the coming of the Son of Man, but if they are at all authentic, as Dodd thinks they are, it is difficult to see how the sudden appearance of the *master* or the *bridegroom* is comparable to the persecution or other *disasters* for which the disciples—in Dodd's theory—were cautioned to stand ready. Does Dodd mean that the "crisis" confronting Jesus' hearers consisted only in the threat of practical or political consequences? Or was the crisis of decision occasioned by the appearance of the "eternal order"? Dodd does not always make it clear what he means by "crisis," or what he thinks occasioned it. It would seem more likely, as Schweitzer and Bultmann propose, to draw the conclusion that the urgency or crisis of repentance and decision arose out of the conviction expressed in Jesus' parables and other teaching alike, that the Kingdom of God, Son of Man, and judgment had drawn near.

Dodd is, evidently, embarrassed by the fact that he is unable to account for all of Jesus' eschatological language through the theories of realized eschatology and symbolic imagery. Despite his resolve to renounce the literary solution, he proposes that much of the futuristic evidence is to be attributed to the church after all: for instance, the parable of the talents (Matt. 25:14–30 = Luke 19:12–27);[39] and, in fact, wherever else futuristic eschatology may be found in the Synoptic Gospels, since (in Dodd's judgment) "the earliest tradition of the teaching of Jesus" is characterized by "realized eschatology."[40] Dodd's insistence that the Kingdom came fully in Jesus' ministry compels him, on finding the expression "until the kingdom of God comes" (Luke 22:18), to put Luke in the impossible position of attributing to Jesus belief in a "*second* 'coming' of the Kingdom of God."[41] There is no evidence, however, to suggest that either Jesus or Luke expected the Kingdom of God to come *twice*. The more probable explanation of Luke 22:18 is that here Luke reports Jesus' expectation that the Kingdom of God would soon come.

Some passages Dodd simply overlooks or ignores. For instance, he discusses Matt. 10:17–22, but passes over v. 23 without comment.[42] He considers Luke 10:9–11 evidence for realized eschatology, but disregards v. 12, which clearly implies the futurity of "that day."[43] As still another method of circumventing the problem, he declares that since the idea of realized eschatology is not paralleled in Jewish literature, it is here that "the *differentia* of the teaching of Jesus upon the Kingdom of God" must be found.[44] This suggestion echoes Harnack's distinction between "what is traditional and what is peculiar, between kernel and husk."

Dodd considers Jesus' proclamation of the coming judgment, like the coming Kingdom, only symbolical, a kind of homiletic stratagem: "The time-honoured image of a Last Judgment is simply assumed, and used to give vividness and force to solemn warnings."[45] Dodd sometimes explains that this symbolism was intended to represent the nature of reality in a "moral universe" where wrongdoing and goodness result in fitting consequences.[46] In *The Parables,* however, Dodd subsumes the coming of judgment under realized eschatology: men pass judgment *upon themselves* by their attitude to Jesus and his appeal. There is to be no future judgment.[47]

In Dodd's view, Jesus conceived neither the Kingdom nor the time of judgment as future events or eras. Jesus used apocalyptic language to express some other spiritual or otherworldly meaning, or else was referring to forthcoming political-historical (but not eschatological) events which he saw looming on the horizon, or else such language was improperly attributed to Jesus by the early community. Dodd apparently does not believe it possible that Jesus actually could have shared the eschatological ideas of his contemporaries.

The Teaching and Example of Jesus: The Ideal Morality of the Realized Kingdom of God, and Its Modern Relevance

Like Schweitzer, Dodd denies that Jesus' teaching was meant as an "ideal for conduct in an ideally perfect society," for in such a society there would be no occasion to turn the other cheek.[48] But it was not an interim ethic either. Instead, Dodd says, it is the way men live who are already in the presence of the Kingdom of God:

> It is the absolute ethic of the Kingdom of God, the moral principles of a new order of life. The implied major premise of all His ethical sayings is the affirmation "The Kingdom of God has come upon you." . . .
>
> This affirmation is the major premise of all the ethical precepts of the Gospels. They set forth the manner in which men will respond if they know that the eternal God confronts them in His Kingdom, power and glory, upon the common ways of life. . . . Many of the ethical precepts—and those the most characteristic—are conceived as imaginative pictures of the kind of action which is appropriate—in its quality and in its direction—to those who know that human life is lived directly under the reign of God.[49]

Jesus did not lay down rules, or even general principles; instead, he spoke to concrete situations. His teaching is characterized by "concrete and particularized precepts."

> Indeed, it is only when He was challenged directly to define the "first and greatest commandment" that He allowed Himself so broad a generalization as "Thou shalt love the Lord thy God with all thy heart, and thy neighbor as thyself."[50]

Jesus' "precepts" or "maxims" were meant as "dramatic illustrations" of a "consistent understanding of God, man and the world, which is the background and presupposition of ethical action."[51] They reveal, therefore, the "absolute standards" of the Kingdom of God.

> These standards, however, are not defined in general and abstract propositions, but in dramatic pictures of action in concrete situations; and they are intended to appeal to the conscience by way of the imagination.[52]

Jesus' teachings or precepts have their modern relevance, then, by way of imagination or analogy, as one perceives the similarity between one's own situation and that of Jesus' hearers or stories. The precepts were intended not as laws but as examples. Sometimes, however, Dodd refers to these standards as "the Law of Christ" which "may be stated in the form of His own New Commandment—'love one another, as I have loved you.' "[53] The love of God is manifested in the work of Jesus Christ, whose behavior in certain situations provides "a model of the right way to behave in such situations," and whose coming into the world as a "poor man" and going to death in complete obedience to the will of God reveals the character of God himself.[54] God's love is the basic pattern for ethical response as set forth in Jesus' teaching as well:

> The several precepts, therefore, may be regarded as examples of the way in which divine charity may become effective in various relations and situations occurring in the course of our lives. The standard of reference is always the love of God.[55]

Jesus' life and teachings both exemplify the "eternal nature of God," and it is this "eternal nature" that is the source of all moral obligation.[56] God's eternal nature, of course, has not changed since the time of Jesus; his life and teachings are, therefore, as relevant today as in his own time. The Christian life, or life under the "reign" of God, consists in obedience to the standard of God's nature, specifically, of his love, revealed in Jesus and his precepts.

> I suggest that we may regard each of the precepts as indicating, in a dramatic picture of some actual situation, the *quality* and *direction* of action which shall conform to the standard set by the divine *agapē*.[57]

Though Dodd retains the expression "the Kingdom of God," it has no real place in his interpretation of either Jesus' teaching or Christian ethics. What is important is the "eternal nature of God"; the standard for Christian moral life is the love of God exemplified in Jesus and his precepts.

Dodd finds Jesus' ethical teaching to have a twofold function in the Christian life. First, it is to be thought of as "providing the material for an intelligent act of 'repentance' " in that it discloses the "absolute standards" of the Kingdom of

God. In this situation, men are challenged to decision: to repent and believe the gospel. We cannot fulfill these absolute standards, "and yet, since God is here in His Kingdom, these standards are obligatory"; the precepts of Jesus therefore judge us, "expose our need for forgiveness and throw us back upon the inexhaustible mercy of God which offers such forgiveness."[58] Forgiveness is "the actual creative power of God coming in His Kingdom" which is released "when men accept His judgment and repent." Thereby, "unlimited possibilities" of obedient response are opened up.[59] The grace of God thus "places us within His Kingdom" and "becomes a source of moral power towards the attainment of" the absolute ethic of the Kingdom set forth in Jesus' teaching.[60] Dodd's use of the first person plural here and elsewhere makes it clear that he understands Jesus' teaching or precepts to have an immediate contemporary relevance. Since he takes the position that Jesus believed the Kingdom to have come with his own ministry, and (presumably) that it has been present ever since, he evidently understands that Jesus' precepts were *intended* not only for his own contemporaries but for all times and places, thus also for us.

Once men are "within the Kingdom," the second function of Jesus' ethical teaching becomes operative:

> At this point the ethical precepts begin to take on a fresh aspect. They become not only the standards by which our conduct is judged, but guideposts on the way we must travel in seeking the true ends of our being under the Kingdom of God.[61]

By "guideposts" Dodd means two things: on the one hand, an external standard, "a mark we must aim at," or an "ideal standard by which our conduct is to be tested and judged."[62] On the other hand, Jesus' commandments become, "through reflection and through effort, increasingly a part of our total outlook upon life." The standard of moral judgment or "law of Christ" is thus "written on our hearts." When that has happened, Jesus' precepts "will find expression in action appropriate to the changing situation in which we find ourselves."[63] Dodd proposes to interpret Jesus' teaching, in effect, as "situation ethics"; but in the situation, one is informed by the "guideposts" of Jesus' precepts.

Jesus proclaimed the absolute or ideal standard of morality: the ethics of the realized Kingdom of God. This standard drives men to repentance, for they see how short they have fallen of God's demand. But those who repent are forgiven and given new powers of obedience. For them, the standard becomes a challenge to new obedience, and an internal attitude or outlook on life. Nevertheless, Dodd says, Jesus did not expect that even those "in the Kingdom" would be able to fulfill his demands completely.

> His precepts indicate, in vivid pictures, the *quality,* and the *direction,* of any action which is to conform to the love of God. This quality may be present, in its degree, at quite a lowly level of performance, and the right direction may be clearly discernible in the act even though the goal is still far off.[64]

The expression "quality and direction" is characteristic of Dodd's discussions of the intention and relevance of Jesus' ethical teaching. Dodd insists that the demands of "Christ's law" can never be satisfied. "At each level the precepts are obligatory. At no level, even the highest attained by man on earth, are they exhaustively fulfilled. There is always a challenge in them."[65] Dodd does not deny that the standard of obedience that Jesus required was absolute, but his proposal that the "quality and direction" of action demanded by Jesus may be present at "quite lowly levels of performance" dilutes the radical character of the demand. Dodd does not insist as forcefully as Bultmann that in each situation Jesus' demand confronts man with an Either-Or, a decision to obey God or else become disobedient. Dodd emphasizes the possibility of some limited obedience more than the demand for radical, unlimited obedience.

Dodd states more explicitly than Bultmann, however, that

Jesus' ethical teaching is relevant to the situation of the modern Christian. It is easier for him to do so, because of his confidence in the theory of realized eschatology. For Bultmann, as for Schweitzer, Jesus expected the coming of the Kingdom as an imminent event. In Dodd's conception, there is no gap between the historical Jesus with his world view and expectations and the Jesus whose life and ethical teaching provide a moral standard for modern Christians. Jesus believed that the Kingdom had already come: men already lived under the reign of God. Men today still live, in Dodd's view, in or under the reign or Kingdom of God. The standard of ethical response set forth in Jesus' example and teaching has, therefore, the same significance today that it had for Jesus and his immediate hearers.

Evaluation

Dodd's interpretation of the significance of Jesus' teaching for the Christian life makes a genuine contribution. Like Bultmann, he appreciates the particularity and concreteness of Jesus' ethical teaching: he does not attempt to reduce it to principles or generalities. His references to Jesus' "precepts" imply a series of such general principles, but he does not identify or specify the substance of these precepts. Generally, Dodd sees the underlying theme of Jesus' message in terms of the Johannine "new commandment": "Love one another, as I have loved you." His proposal that the "quality and direction" of life demanded in particular precepts of Jesus can serve to test our conduct in analogous situations indicates at least one way in which Jesus' teaching may function in connection with the ethical decisions of his latter-day disciples, whether Jesus intended these precepts for later generations or not. Likewise, his idea that Jesus' teaching may be built into an internal standard of moral judgment which then comes to expression in response to particular situations is a more adequate representation of the nature of ethical decision than the existentialist conception that moral decision takes place "in empty space," or the situationist supposition that the situation itself discloses what is to be done.

The question arises, however, whether Dodd has adequately handled the evidence that Jesus expected the Kingdom, Son of Man, and judgment to appear imminently as decisive eschatological happenings. Dodd insists that Jesus' eschatological language was "symbolic." But is this more than a slight variation of the liberal assumption that Jesus did not *really* mean it when he used apocalyptic language? Certainly all language is symbolic. But did Jesus mean by it to represent an "eternal order beyond time and space," or the coming of God's Kingdom and judgment in very concrete, temporal, spatial, and inescapable form? There is no evidence that Jesus thought in terms of the former (Platonic) categories.

Dodd's further proposals—that such sayings as *appear* eschatological in fact referred to historical-political events which Jesus foresaw, or were added by the church, or at any rate, are not important since the *differentia* of his teaching is "realized eschatology"—in common reflect an a priori determination by Dodd to eliminate futuristic eschatology from Jesus' teaching and thought.

In treating the significance of Jesus' teaching, Dodd does not distinguish between Jesus' intention and the relevance of his teaching. For Dodd, there is no real difference, and thus no need for interpretation: in Jesus and his teaching, God and his Kingdom confront us with the same demands, the same moral standard that confronted Jesus' hearers—the morality of the realized Kingdom of God. There is no problem about interim ethics or "rewards," or about Jesus' being mistaken in his expectations. There is nothing strange about Jesus or his world view that requires demythologizing. There is no gap between the historical Jesus and the Jesus whom Dodd finds in the kerygma. Significantly, Dodd does not speak of a new "quest of the historical Jesus," but rather of resuming the "unfinished quest."[66] Dodd presents valid insights with respect to the nature and significance of Jesus' ethical teaching. But his treatment of eschatology must be rejected as exegetically and historically untenable. If Jesus did believe that the eschatological Kingdom of God was about to arrive, it need not follow, however, as Dodd apparently fears, that he and his teaching must lose their meaning and authority for us. However, the way in which that authority and meaning can be understood would have to be seen somewhat differently from the way Dodd interprets it.

Other British and American Interpreters

C. H. Dodd has certainly been the most influential of the modern British interpreters of Jesus and his message. He also represents the more theologically liberal, if critically conservative, tendencies of Anglo-Saxon New Testament scholarship generally. Some recent British and American writers, of course, have accepted Dodd's conclusions only in part, or even rejected them entirely. There is considerable divergence of opinion both with regard to the character of Jesus and his teaching, and to the manner in which his and/or its relevance is to be understood. The four major positions examined, those of Harnack, Schweitzer, Bultmann, and Dodd, can serve as points of reference in reviewing these recent Anglo-Saxon interpretations.

Modern Motifs and Liberalism: Optimism and Realized Eschatology

Many of these interpretations bear a definite resemblance to earlier Protestant liberalism. In fact, it is difficult in both Britain and America to draw a distinct line between "liberal" and "modern" interpretations. Possibly this is the case because the era of liberalism never came to a decisive end in these countries as it did in Germany under the impact of guilt and defeat in two catastrophic wars.

Protestant liberals characteristically attributed to Jesus their own optimistic appraisal of the nature and destiny of man.

Man was by nature a child of the Father, or even "inherently" good—at any rate, essentially harmless. Jesus had founded the Kingdom of God on earth and called men of all eras to the task of building it with him through social progress in history. The Kingdom of God is immanent; it has entered history. The individual may also enter the Kingdom, Harnack had suggested, in the experience of God's rule in his heart. Such optimism about human nature reappears untamed in such recent American writers as Harvey Cox and Thomas Altizer. The former regards man as God's "partner" in bringing in the Kingdom of God, which he all but equates with the "secular city" or the process of secularization which he discerns as the action of God.[67] Cox does not mention the name of Reinhold Niebuhr in *The Secular City,* let alone show any awareness of the sinful and tragic dimensions of human nature and history. It has been pointed out that he neglects "the Fall" and the crucifixion, and he, himself, notes that his book never mentions death.[68]

If Cox considers man God's partner, Altizer (on the canonical authority of the poet William Blake) declares that God is man and man is God.[69] According to Altizer's Hegelian system of emanations, God negated himself and became Christ; Christ negated himself and has become mankind: he "is actually present in our flesh," thus "manifest in every human hand and face." After the manner of the writers of the "liberal lives," Altizer does not hesitate to ascribe his system to the historical Jesus: "[The] form of faith . . . present in the radical Christian . . . claims to be a recovery and renewal of the original message and person of Jesus."[70] William Hamilton speaks vaguely of the decline of "neo-orthodoxy" and its pessimistic doctrine of man, but offers the assurance that "neo-orthodoxy now doesn't work" because its "pessimism doesn't persuade any more." Now there "not only are no tragedies around . . . but there can't be tragedies" any longer. Hamilton, writing in 1965, looked for a new period of optimism as both a "cause and a consequence" of the death of God.[71] Both Altizer and Hamilton speak disparagingly of Reinhold Niebuhr and "old Niebuhrians," but neither gives any hint that he has understood what Niebuhr has to say.

Archbishop William Temple, though less optimistic than many of his American counterparts in the "social gospel" movement, shared their hope that the Kingdom of God, inaugurated by Christ, might be achieved in history. In a sermon delivered in 1931, he urged, "If we should stream out after Him, there might be a Kingdom of God in Oxford tomorrow."[72] Only a few Anglo-Saxon writers have concurred with Schweitzer's conclusion that Jesus regarded the Kingdom of God as a wholly future, world-transforming event: most notably, Morton S. Enslin.[73] William Manson, John Knox, and Paul Ramsey in general accept the futuristic position, but do not always maintain it consistently.[74]

Some writers manage to discuss Jesus' ethical teaching/preaching without referring to the problem of the Kingdom of God or interim ethics at all. B. H. Branscomb wrote *The Teachings of Jesus* (1931) without visible awareness of the problem, and mentions Schweitzer only once in a list of supplementary readings concerning "what Judas betrayed." Jesus simply taught certain principles and virtues for all men to follow. In a book published the previous year, John Baillie groups Schweitzer with Paul, Francis of Assisi, and Canon Barnett as great men of Christendom, but makes no mention of him, or of the Kingdom of God, or of eschatology in his book on the significance of Jesus. Jesus simply teaches God's "redemptive love."[75] Recently Joseph Fletcher has attributed his theory of "situation ethics" to Jesus without, however, making any reference to eschatology or the Kingdom of God.[76] He mentions Schweitzer only twice, in both instances as author of the aphorism "The good conscience is an invention of the devil."[77]

Interim Ethics, or Ethics for All Times?

Nearly all Anglo-Saxon writers—including, curiously, many who concede that Jesus really did expect the Kingdom to come in the near future—are united in opposition to what they understand (or misunderstand) to be the meaning of Schweitzer's interim ethics interpretation.[78] Most of them have neglected to read Schweitzer carefully (if at all) and suppose him to have understood that Jesus' teaching/preaching was derived solely from his expectation that the Kingdom was near, or that he concluded that Jesus was "deluded" or a "fanatic," and that his message can no longer have any meaning for men of later generations. As has been shown, Schweitzer drew no such conclusions.[79] A great many writers are, apparently, under the impression that Jesus' message can have no significance for later generations, including our own, unless Jesus *intended* his teaching for all times, or for us. E. F. Scott, for instance, insisted that though Jesus expected the Kingdom to come soon, "for His teaching as a whole He claims a permanent value."[80] Other writers in the liberal tradition also were to describe Jesus as a moral philosopher, "inculcating" a certain spirit or set of principles for men of all ages to come.[81] Jesus defines love as caring "for all whom *we* meet on life's road, . . . for all who need *our* help." Jesus shows "*us* what is wrong with *our* living."[82] Even Bishop Robinson speaks of Jesus' immediate concern for us: "Jesus . . . is content with the knowledge that if *we* have the heart of the matter in *us,* if *our* eye is single, then love will find the way."[83]

John Knox insists that the matter is not so simple: Jesus "was not thinking of a continuing history, an indefinitely extended future time. . . . He was not thinking of us or of the centuries which separate our time from his."[84] But then Knox himself continues to speak of Jesus' intentions or concerns for and demands upon "us"![85] M. S. Enslin, who maintains consistently that Jesus expected the Kingdom in the near future, states in characteristically pungent style what must certainly be the case if that contention is correct:

> He [Jesus] was talking to the men and women of that day about his concerns and theirs. He was not talking to us over their heads, pretending an interest in them but really concerned with us.[86]

How, then, can Jesus' words have any authority or relevance for us? Schweitzer himself wrestled with that question, certain that Jesus and his message have direct meaning and authority in our time, but equally convinced that Jesus expected the Kingdom to come within his own lifetime, or shortly after his death. Other interpreters also, especially in Britain and America where the influence of Barth's church and Christ dogmatics was delayed, diffused, and ultimately negligible, continued to preserve the conviction that Jesus and his message are, somehow, the foundation of Christian ethics. Still, as long as Jesus is held to have expected the Kingdom to come in the first century, there remains a seemingly insurmountable barrier between him and his teaching, on the one side, and subsequent history and ourselves on the other. He could not have intended his teaching for us in that case. Furthermore, there is little resemblance between his apocalyptic world view and our own view of history as an indefinite continuum into the future. Also, if he had been wrong in his expectation about the Kingdom of God, perhaps he was mistaken about other matters too. Bultmann, as we have seen, was willing to go along with Barth's judgment that the historical Jesus and his thought are extraneous for theology, which can place its reliance solely upon the kerygmatic Christ. But Bultmann was unwilling to negate the significance of Jesus and his message for ethics. Since Bultmann followed J. Weiss and Schweitzer in the view that Jesus regarded the Kingdom as an entirely future catastrophic event, he chose to rescue Jesus and his message from irrelevancy (to ethics) by converting Jesus' first-century eschatological beliefs into twentieth-century existentialism. Anglo-Saxons, however, have generally tended to be skeptical in the presence of philosophical legerdemain.

At this decisive point C. H. Dodd entered the scene. Anglo-Saxon exegetes and moral philosophers and theologians were waiting for a solution that would make it possible to retain and explain the significance of Jesus and his teaching after all. Dodd had the answer: realized eschatology! If Jesus believed and proclaimed that the Kingdom of God had already come during his lifetime, then these difficulties disappear—at least if one is able to believe that the Kingdom of God really did come with Jesus, and has remained on earth ever since. On closer inspection, however, most Anglo-Saxon writers found that Dodd's theory failed to account for all the evidence. It, too, involved too much philosophical—and also exegetical—legerdemain. Some of the Synoptic evidence could well be interpreted as realized eschatology, but what was left indicated Jesus' belief in a future coming of the Kingdom of God, Son of Man, and judgment. The vast majority of Anglo-Saxon interpreters have attempted, therefore, to occupy some middle position between Schweitzer and Dodd. The evidence has compelled them to recognize that Jesus expected the coming of the Kingdom in the future, but their desire to retain the authority and significance of Jesus and his message encouraged them to interpret such passages as might be susceptible to mean that "in some sense" (a typical phrase in this connection) Jesus also understood the Kingdom of God to be present. Presumably this latter understanding was not mistaken, even if the other was.

Ethics of the Realized Kingdom of God

Two of the most important proponents of such mediating or "both-and" interpretations are T. W. Manson and Amos Wilder. Manson's influence, in turn, is reflected (with J. Jeremias') in Norman Perrin, and (with Dodd's and Vincent Taylor's) in Archibald M. Hunter. Wilder's influence is normative for E. C. Gardner and Harvey Cox. Manson proposed that "the Kingdom of God in its essence is the Reign of God, a personal relation between God and the individual," something eternal, like "the Fatherhood of God."[87] This feature of Manson's interpretation is essentially the same as Harnack's. Perrin, similarly, urges that for Jesus the Kingdom of God, in the final analysis, meant personal religious experience. Jesus' "ethical teaching illustrates the response by means of which men enter ever more fully into this experience."[88] Manson declares that the Kingdom came *"de facto"* during

Jesus' ministry, specifically, in "Peter's Confession: 'Thou art the Messiah.' "[89] No one else has subscribed to that novel conjecture. Manson, also, like Dodd, identified the Kingdom of God with Jesus' ministry, indeed, with Jesus himself.[90] A. M. Hunter follows Manson in this equation or "equivalence," claiming support for it in the Synoptic evidence.[91]

Amos Wilder proposes to differentiate between the "formal" and the "fundamental" or "essential" sanctions invoked by Jesus in connection with his message. Jesus' use of eschatological language was "stylistic" and "imaginative," a pedagogical device employed to "lend credence" or "dramatize" his moral demands for the "unphilosophical minds" of "simple people."[92] The "fundamental" sanction of Jesus' teaching was his experience and conception of the nature of God; his appeal was "to the God-conscious moral nature of his hearers."[93] At the same time, Wilder also maintains that Jesus himself "is . . . the embodiment of the Kingdom," an equation which Harvey Cox presents on Wilder's authority as an established datum: "Jesus *is* the Kingdom."[94] In this dubious proposition, Cox finds "the fullest possible disclosure of the partnership of God and man in history." On the basis of this assertion, Cox sets out upon his quest for the actualization of the Kingdom of God in the secular city. A number of other writers also believe that the Kingdom was present in Jesus' works, words, and/or person: for instance, T. J. J. Altizer, William Barclay, C. J. Cadoux, and John Knox.[95]

Various writers in the liberal tradition assert that the Kingdom is present wherever men fulfill or obey the will of God.[96] Manson and Wilder prefer to put the matter the other way around: Jesus' ethical teachings set forth what God desires as the moral response of those who are already in the Kingdom of God. They agree, basically, with Dodd, that Jesus' ethics is the ethics of the realized Kingdom of God. Thus Manson writes, "The ideal picture of human life which Jesus draws in what he says about morals, is a picture of life in the Kingdom of God on earth." The teaching sets forth illustrations, examples, or "samples of the fruit" of the transformed life.[97]

Similarly, Wilder describes Jesus' ethic as "an ethic of the present Kingdom of God" or "time of salvation" when Jesus' hearers are now in a position to respond to the call "for 'fruits worthy of repentance,' i.e., conduct evidencing the changed disposition."[98] Neither Manson nor Wilder believes that Jesus' expectation and proclamation of the *coming* Kingdom was of any real significance in connection with his ethics. His hearers were to repent because of their experience of the *nature* of God, "as Jesus reveals Him, that is, as the merciful loving Father who seeks and saves the lost."[99] As in Harnack's understanding, it was the eternal nature of God, not the coming Kingdom of God, that Jesus proclaimed as the occasion for repentance. Such a message could just as well have omitted any reference to the future coming of the Kingdom. Hunter and Perrin present essentially the same conclusion.[100]

On the assumption (normally taken for granted rather than defended) that the Kingdom of God which came with Jesus has remained on earth (in some form or other) since Jesus' departure, many of these writers are prepared to suppose that Jesus' words are as valid and relevant to us as they were to his contemporaries. The writers who characterize Jesus' ethics as "the ethics of the realized Kingdom of God" do not, therefore, ordinarily proceed to inquire as to its relevance in the modern world, or as to the nature of the moral life. Since the Kingdom of God is, presumably, still present, they evidently assume that Jesus' "ethics of the realized Kingdom" can be taken over in our time without further ado. Another significant feature of their interpretation is that they generally present Jesus as a relatively placid guide or portrayer of a "standard," "direction," or "illustration" of ideal behavior, rather than as an "imperious ruler" (Schweitzer) demanding radical obedience (Bultmann).

Ethics and the Coming Kingdom

On the other hand, those writers who propose that Jesus really believed that the Kingdom was coming, and proclaimed this as a matter of serious consequence to his hearers, tend to describe Jesus' teaching/preaching in terms of *demand,* a demand that retains its authority for us in spite or because of his eschatological beliefs. Enslin, for example, urges that far from being inconsequential in his own time or irrelevant now, Jesus "stands ever demanding from his followers the same commitment and devotion to their tasks which he brought to his."[101] So also William Manson:

> Jesus was not speaking of higher or lower values or levels of life in any general sense. He was speaking of the coming of the *Kingdom of God* at the earliest moment as the one critical issue of life. . . . Nevertheless, the demand has relation to man's true life under any conceivable set of conditions, and thus it has continued to lay its imperative on the church. . . . The principle then was, and remains, that it is not through simple improvement or increase in knowledge or ethical insight that the way of the Christian disciples lies, but through *obedience,* commitment, surrender, the taking of the yoke of Jesus.[102]

John Knox and Paul Ramsey both find in Jesus' apocalyptic message "the absolute, pure will of God without compromise in view of the conditions of human life and without concessions to human finitude and sin."[103] Both acknowledge their indebtedness to Martin Dibelius' treatment of Jesus' ethic as the pure will of God which was to obtain in the *future* Kingdom of God, but both reject Dibelius' position which renders that ethic irrelevant in the present period before the coming of the Kingdom. Both also reject the only apparent alternative, namely, that Jesus meant his teaching/preaching as an "ethic for the interim," until the Kingdom should come. Ramsey insists that "*genesis* has nothing to do with *validity,*" so that the truth of Jesus' ethic has not perished with the apocalyptic world view. Moreover, precisely *because* Jesus did not take into account "prudential calculations of consequences" or a person's "sober regard for the future performance of his responsibility for family or friends" or the fact that *"there is always more than one neighbor,"* Ramsey declares that "Jesus' ethic gained an absolute validity transcending limitations to this or that place or time or civilization." All other neighbors, Ramsey says, "were apocalyptically removed from view." Only the single neighbor remained.[104] Knox's position is essentially the same:

> Jesus as an ethical teacher belongs to all the generations just because he did not, in a sense, belong to his own. That is, the knowledge that he stood at or just before the final crisis of history allowed for a preoccupation with the absolute righteousness more complete and intensive than in ordinary circumstances might, humanly speaking, have been possible. If this is true, instead of blaming eschatology for the "impracticableness" of Jesus' ethical teaching, we should thank eschatology for that teaching's majesty and permanent relevance.[105]

Ramsey himself poses the obvious question: "There is no such situation in a non-apocalyptic world. How, then, can this ethic mean anything at all for actual practice?"[106] Ramsey and Knox find Jesus' ethic theoretically but not practically relevant. It remains, in R. Niebuhr's phrase, "an impossible possibility." Nevertheless, these men who stress the futurity of God's Kingdom for Jesus, like Schweitzer and Bultmann, succeed in preserving the sense of authority, the imperative quality of Jesus' teaching/preaching, even if they do not explicate its relevance. The advocates of "the ethics of the realized Kingdom," on the other hand, at least theoretically are in a position to assume the practical relevance of Jesus' ethics, but generally lose the sense of absolute moral obligation or demand.[107]

The Significance of Jesus and His Message

A number of other proposals have been made by recent Anglo-Saxon interpreters by way of accounting for the sense of moral authority and relevance which Jesus and his message continue to evoke in our time. Some of these interpretations focus primarily upon Jesus himself; others, more upon his message.

1. THE ETHICS OF "THE MAN FOR OTHERS." Bonhoeffer's characterization of Jesus as "the man for others" has been picked up by several writers as the essence of the matter. J. A. T. Robinson, who takes the term as a chapter heading in *Honest to God,* understands it as the meaning of the incarnation, life, and death of Jesus: "Jesus is the 'man for others,' the one in whom Love has completely taken over, the one who is utterly open to, and united with, the Ground of his being."[108] He also understands it as the clue to the meaning of the Christian life, specifically, of Paul's (and also Paul Tillich's) conception of "the new creation" or "the new man 'in Christ Jesus' ": "It is nothing peculiarly religious. . . . It is the life of 'the man for others,' the love whereby we are brought completely into one with the Ground of our being, manifesting itself in the unreconciled relationships of our existence."[109] Had Robinson been familiar with the thought of H. R. Niebuhr, particularly his conceptions of "radical monotheism" and "relational value theory," he might have developed this clue still more precisely.

Paul van Buren is not, apparently, acquainted with these conceptions of Niebuhr's either, but approximates them, interestingly, especially in his chapter "Jesus of Nazareth." Jesus was not only a free man, free for his neighbor, but also the liberator of other men, freeing them to be for others also: "The Gospel . . . is the good news of a free man who has set other men free, first proclaimed by those to whom this had happened. And it has happened again and again during nineteen centuries."[110] Van Buren's analysis of the origin and nature of faith closely resembles H. Richard Niebuhr's.[111] Van Buren uses R. M. Hare's category, "blik" or "point of orientation" (which Ian Ramsey describes as arising out of "a situation of discernment or disclosure, a situation which is seen suddenly in a new way demanding a commitment of the viewer"), to indicate the significance of the "history of the Jesus of Nazareth" and Easter for faith.[112] Niebuhr described faith as a double relationship between the believer and the object of faith (whether God or gods), in which the believer finds the ultimate meaning and value of and for his life in his relationship with that object, and responds to it with commitment or loyalty. Radical monotheistic faith, faith in God who is the ground or source and center of all being, meaning, and value, entails the dethronement or relativizing of all lesser objects of faith or centers of value, including the tribal or "henotheistic" gods, e.g., of clan, caste, or race. All companions in being are now perceived to be good; indeed, "whatever is, is good," but relatively good, no longer as ultimate or absolute centers of value, trust, or loyalty, for there is only One who is absolutely good. Similarly, van Buren writes:

> For the Christian . . . [the] assertion "Jesus is Lord" expresses the fact that Jesus has become his point of orientation, with the consequence that he is freed from acknowledging final loyalty to his nation, family, church, or any other person, and is liberated for service to these other centers of relative loyalty. Because he sees not only his own history but the history of all men in the light of the one history of Jesus of Nazareth and Easter, he will not rest content when his nation, family, or church seek to live only for themselves; he will try to get them in the service of others.[113]

Though it is God, not Jesus, who is the "Lord," "point of orientation," "object of faith," or "center of value" for Niebuhr's radical monotheism, Niebuhr bears testimony to the significance of Jesus as the one in whom radical (monotheistic) faith was incarnate, whose life and message mediate such faith to many Christians.

2. ETHICS AS THE FORM OF CHRIST IN NEIGHBOR AND SELF. William Hamilton also finds a clue to the significance of Jesus for the moral life in Bonhoeffer's thought—not in his concept of Jesus as the man for others, but in the combination of Bonhoeffer's earlier idea that the "form of Christ" is in history, taking form in man and the world, so that the world and man are in Christ (realized eschatology), and Bonhoeffer's later correction or repudiation of such optimism in his statement that "man is challenged to participate in the sufferings of God at the hands of a godless world." The Lordship of Jesus has "the

form of suffering and service and hiddenness."[114] And yet, Christ is in the world: he is "concealed in the world, in the neighbor, in this struggle for justice, in that struggle for beauty, clarity, order." The task of the Christian is to discern and serve "Jesus in your neighbor," as Jesus described it in Matt. 25:40. The "world, worldly life, and the neighbor" are "the bearer[s] of the worldly Jesus." The parable of the good Samaritan suggests to Hamilton "another form of the presence of Jesus Christ in the world." "Don't look for Jesus out there . . . —become Jesus. Become a Christ to your neighbor, as Luther put it."[115]

Thomas Altizer owes more to Blake than to Bonhoeffer for his proclamation that Jesus is present "only in the body of a broken and suffering humanity."

Altizer, or perhaps it is Blake—one is often unsure which is supposed to be speaking—states that "Man is Love," and that "truly to pronounce his [Jesus'] name is to give oneself to Jesus as he is manifest in the weak and broken ones about us." The awareness that Jesus is present in the neighbor, indeed, "that Jesus *is* the 'Universal Humanity,' " does not, however, lead Altizer to develop a moral theory in consequence of his commitment to this center of value. Instead of making explicit the ethics of neighbor-love implicit in this view of humanity, Altizer, following the way of Blake and oriental mysticism, is more interested in "the goal of becoming identical with Jesus," Blake's "Great Humanity Divine."[116] Ethics is swallowed up in mysticism.

H. Richard Niebuhr had anticipated Hamilton's account of the "form of Jesus Christ" in the neighbor and the moral self:

> [Christians] know themselves to be Christians when they see their companions in need in the form of Christ; there echoes in their memories in such moments the story Christ told which ended in the well-known statement, "Inasmuch as you have done it to one of these least of these my brethren you have done it unto me."

Again Jesus Christ is the symbolic form with which the self understands itself, with the aid of which it guides and forms itself in its actions and its sufferings. . . . [There are] all the symbolic statements of those Christians who think of and, in part, conduct their lives as imitations of Christ, as conformities to his mind; who follow him, are his disciples, live, suffer, and die with him.[117]

3. THE ETHICS OF RADICAL FAITH: UNIVERSAL RESPONSIBILITY. Whether in discerning Christ in the neighbor, or in imitation of Christ in response to his words "Follow me," Christians find, as Niebuhr puts it, "there echoes in their memories" various words of Jesus spoken to his own generation, but perceived as appropriate to particular situations in which these later would-be disciples find themselves. These sayings may not have been meant as rules or principles for later generations, but the words themselves somehow seem to convey the authority of the speaker across the centuries. Niebuhr suggests that the authority and relevance of such sayings arise out of the perception that our situation is essentially the same as that of Jesus' contemporaries. To be sure, Jesus was mistaken in his philosophy of history, yet this matters little: "He was not dealing with history at all in the first place, but with God, the Lord of time and space."[118] What was important in Jesus' ethical sayings was not "the time factor" so much as "the God-factor." In any case, Niebuhr finds in Jesus the "incarnation of radical faith": both in his life and in his words, Jesus affirms that in all being and activity, there is present the divine intention "that is wholly affirmative of what it brings into being." The Christian who shares this faith perceives every particular being as a companion in being, whose well-being is now a matter of consequence. Responsibility is the mode of the Christian life: "The Christian ethos so uniquely exemplified in Christ himself is an ethics of universal responsibility."[119]

4. THE ETHICS OF LOVE IN THE SITUATION: RELATIONAL ETHICS. Most other Anglo-Saxon interpreters have urged that the essence of the ethics of Jesus and/or of the Christian life is "love." In the older "liberal" tradition it was taken for granted that "the fundamental moral law is, 'Thou shalt love thy neighbor as thyself.' "[120] Some were not quite sure whether

love is a "commandment," a "precept," a "principle," or an "attitude." The meaning or character of love is still notoriously uncertain. The centrality of *agape* ("love") has been emphasized by a great many writers, several of whom, strangely, place the accent on the final syllable (thus, *agape'*)—a small point, but symbolic of the confusion that obtains with respect to the shape of love.[121] Recently "love" has been rediscovered by certain adherents of the so-called "new morality" or "situation ethics."

Joseph Fletcher speaks of love as if it were *itself* "the highest good": *"Only one thing is intrinsically good, namely, love: nothing else,"* Fletcher insists.[122] Unfortunately, he does not describe the nature or function of love, but is content to hypostatize it. Bishop Robinson also tends to hypostatize love, probably under the influence of Fletcher whose article in the *Harvard Divinity Bulletin* (1959) he cites as authoritative: Love is the only absolute in the Christian life; to it the Christian must be "totally committed." Nothing is prescribed "—except love." No matter what the situation, "love will find the way." Conversely, "nothing can of itself always be labelled as 'wrong,'" e.g., divorce or sex relations before marriage, "for the only intrinsic evil is lack of love."[123] On the other hand, Robinson occasionally indicates an awareness that love is not a thing in itself after all, but has its meaning in relationships between persons. He parts company with Fletcher precisely at this point, where he notices that it is not *love*, or *the situation*, but *the person* (*or persons*) in the situation that is of consequence: "It [love] alone can afford to be utterly open to the situation, *or rather to the person in the situation,* uniquely and for his own sake, without losing its direction or unconditionality." Moral norms, he goes on, interpreting and again (perhaps unconsciously) correcting Fletcher, "must be defended, as Fletcher puts it, 'situationally, not prescriptively'—in other words, in terms of the fact that *persons* matter, and the deepest *welfare of these particular persons in this particular situation* matters."[124]

Before the term "situation ethics" was invented, Paul Ramsey had also advanced its basic insight, which he found in the actions and sayings of Jesus: "Jesus quite spontaneously left the rules behind in order quickly to take maximum care of those in need." Christians, who take seriously his example, "are bound by Jesus' attitude of sticking as close as possible to human need, no matter what the rules say." The meaning of love is indicated in Jesus' words "as yourself" (Mark 12:31): "You naturally love yourself for your own sake." Christian love has to do, therefore, with the objective well-being of the neighbor, not with "feeling" or emotion: "The commandment requires the Christian to aim at his neighbor's good just as unswervingly as man by nature wishes his own."[125] A. M. Hunter also describes the character of love with precision:

> By love Jesus does not mean some kind of sentimental emotion; neither does he mean that we must resolve to *like* certain people. (In this sense we cannot love to order.) Love, as Jesus defines it in saying and parable, means "caring"—caring, practically and persistently, for all whom we meet on life's road.[126]

As John Knox points out, love or "caring" is not a matter of duty. When we act generously toward ourselves, we are not performing a duty, but doing what we want to do. "Caring" means just that: the concern for the other persons, the desire for their well-being, which expresses itself in appropriate action (or restraint).[127] H. Richard Niebuhr does not analyze "love" as such in his essay on "relational value theory."[128] Had he done so, it is likely that he would have agreed with these writers who find it neither an "absolute" or "intrinsic" good, nor a subjective "feeling," but a relational category, in effect, "concern for the well-being of my companion in being."

CHAPTER V

Jesus, Ethics, and the Present Situation

NOT EVEN the most radical literary and form critics doubt that it is possible to obtain from the Synoptic sources a probable account of the character and content of Jesus' teaching/preaching. The central problem is that Jesus' message appears in connection with his expectation that history was in its last days, that the Kingdom of God, Son of Man, and time of judgment would soon come.

THE PROBLEM OF UNREALIZED ESCHATOLOGY

It has been difficult for most interpreters both to believe that Jesus actually expected these events and intended his message for his contemporaries living in the interim before their occurrence, and at the same time to believe that Jesus' message can be relevant and authoritative for the moral life in the modern world. These writers are generally convinced that Jesus and his teaching do have some such relevance and authority. Rather than sacrifice this conviction at the altar of historical criticism, many of them prefer to believe that Jesus must have *meant* his message for all times, or for us, or to look for some way to detach Jesus' message from its eschatological context. Harnack and Schweitzer adopt the latter strategy. Bultmann and Dodd, on the other hand, attempt to translate the eschatological world view into some more congenial philosophy, respectively, existentialism and Platonism.

Dodd also maintains that Jesus thought that the Kingdom of God had already come. Many, especially Anglo-Saxon, writers concur, though with the reservation that Jesus *also* expected it to come in the future. The dogmatic interest of many such interpreters is evident in their tendency to stress the present aspect of the Kingdom and to deemphasize, or even ignore, its future coming. It seems, generally, to be feared that if Jesus really expected the imminent arrival of the Kingdom, his teaching could have no more meaning for us since (1) he would not, then, have *intended* his teaching "for us"; (2) he would have been mistaken, and his authority would thus be placed in doubt; and (3) we in the twentieth century do not share this expectation, and thus his message would be irrelevant to our situation. Like Harnack, many recent writers have also attempted to circumvent these difficulties by discounting the evidence with respect to Jesus' eschatological perspective "in an effort to identify completely the historical Jesus with the interpretation of his teaching held to be ethically and religiously valid for our time."[1] What can be said about these "difficulties"?

First, it must simply be recognized that Jesus did not, so far as we can tell from the Synoptic evidence, intend his message for later generations, centuries, or us. This does not, however, mean automatically that his message can have no meaning for us. If what Jesus had to say about the character of God and man and their mutual or triadic relationship (God-self-neighbor) was true in the first century, it is not invalidated by the fact that God, man, and neighbor have continued to confront one another in succeeding centuries, unless the nature of God or the nature of man has changed substantially. There is no evidence that such change has occurred. Jesus may not have intended his sayings and parables for us, but we are not precluded from seeing in them examples or "dramatic pictures of action in concrete situations" arising out of a "consistent understanding of God, man, and the world" which "appeal to the conscience by way of imagination."[2] As H. R. Niebuhr pointed out, Jesus' words echo in our memories as we perceive analogies between the concrete situations in which we encounter our neighbors and the situations, actions, and admonitions presented in the traditions attributed to Jesus. It is interesting to notice, for instance, how many interpreters find meaning and authority in Jesus' words from Matt. 25:40, "As you did it to one of the least of these my brethren, you did it to me," or in his story of the Samaritan who "proved neighbor" to the injured traveler (Luke 10:25–37).

With respect to the second point, it must be admitted without reservation that Jesus was mistaken. The Kingdom of God simply did not come, certainly not in the form that he expected and announced that it would. Even if it could be shown, exegetically, that Jesus did think that the Kingdom had come, we would still have to conclude that he was mistaken, for there is no evidence that it did come, either in or during his ministry, or subsequently. Attempts have been made to locate its immanence in the world. Harnack thought that it was present as God's rule in men's hearts. The "social gospel" theologians saw it present (if only partially realized) in social progress. Dodd suggests that it is present in recurrent celebrations of the Eucharist.[3] Bultmann thinks it present in every recurrent existential crisis of decision in response to preaching (the Protestant sacrament). It is clear, however, if the historical experience of the past twenty centuries has any weight, that the Kingdom of God has not yet come on earth. History reveals the ambivalent character of human nature and destiny. At every level of achievement, as Reinhold Niebuhr puts it, man may and does actualize both his creative and his destructive vitalities. The history of twenty centuries does not justify complete pessimism or moral cynicism and paralysis, of which Reinhold Niebuhr is sometimes, inaccurately, accused.[4] On the other hand, history does not justify the naïve optimism of those who think that the Kingdom of God can be made to appear if only we put Reinhold Niebuhr back on the shelf unopened, half read, or forgotten, and think only positive thoughts about man's nature and destiny, as in the case of Altizer, Cox, Fletcher, and Hamilton.

Jesus was mistaken in believing that the ambiguities of historical existence were about to be resolved in ultimate judgment and redemption. But his understanding as to what God requires and desires of man is not thereby discredited.

The third difficulty needs to be taken seriously: we do not share Jesus' (and the early church's) expectation that the arrival of the Kingdom and Messiah are imminent. If we visualize the end of history in the form of man-made cataclysm, it has more the appearance of Amos' "day of Yahweh" than Jesus' "good news" of the coming of the Kingdom. Our optimism takes the form of hoping that the world as we know it—improved, perhaps, by temporary "proximate" solutions—will be permitted to continue indefinitely into the future. In that case, however, the radical sayings of Jesus about selling all and giving to the poor, or taking no thought for the morrow, however "sublime," cannot be followed responsibly, even if he meant them to be obeyed literally. Furthermore, our historical-political situation is now different from that of Jesus' hearers, who lacked the freedom and responsibility of participating in making the policy decisions of the Roman government. Democracy has given us responsibility for the decisions and indecisions of government which affect the well-being of fellow citizens and fellow humans of other nations. We can no longer hide behind the Pauline-Lutheran illusion that God governs directly and unambiguously through the imperial or national regime. Furthermore, through our natural resources and technology we have become, in David Potter's phrase, a "people of plenty." Now we find not only the local Lazarus sitting at our gate but also the traditionally ignored or exploited "peasant village masses" of the world.[5] Our meager paternalistic interest in both draws us increasingly into a quandary, because of our gradually awakening consciousness that they, most ungratefully, suppose that there is some correlation between their plight and our prosperity. If Jesus did not have us and our complicated situation in view, he cannot have meant his teaching for us, or even understood our problems. How, then, could his message be relevant to our modern situation?

The Significance of Jesus' Ethics in the Modern Situation

All the modern interpreters except Dodd, who does not discuss the subject, maintain on the one hand that Jesus did not intend his teaching as a program of social reform, and on the other, that his teaching is, nevertheless, relevant to the conditions of human life in society. Harnack and Bultmann agreed that Jesus' commandment of love is "profoundly socialistic," or, at least, "may have far-reaching implications for national and social life." Both, however, tended to stress the God-soul relationship to the exclusion of the self-neighbor-world dimension. Harnack's description of the Kingdom as "God and the soul, the soul and its God" includes no mention of the neighbor. Bultmann considers the basic moral question to be, "How can I achieve my true self?"[6] In this view of ethics, as in the medieval quest for the *visio Dei,* the neighbor comes only incidentally or instrumentally into view. Schweitzer has little to say about the social relevance of Jesus' ethic; yet more than the others, he was explicitly concerned for the fate of society, indeed, of civilization. In his two-volume *Philosophy of Civilization,* he undertook to elaborate a world-affirming philosophy, "reverence for life," which could serve to redeem civilization from the doom toward which it was evidently bound. He did not attempt, however, to base "reverence for life" on Jesus' message, though twice, in passing, he attributed it to Jesus. Rather, he sought its basis in mysticism and/or "elemental thinking." In his work as a physician, Schweitzer undertook to do what one man could for the well-being of thousands of diseased men, women, and children in the Congo. Obedience to Jesus' ethic of love or "active self-devotion to others" was not only something Schweitzer wrote about; he "reduplicated" it in his own life.

None of these men, however, develops a social ethic or strategy for resolving, either ultimately or proximately, the problems of man's life in society. Perhaps this fact is no accident. It is not possible to devise a theory of social ethics from

Jesus' teaching or commands alone. Each of the four major interpreters does make a distinctive contribution toward an understanding of the significance of Jesus and his ethics for the moral life, but in each case that contribution needs to be supplemented by other considerations.

Harnack offers, as one expression of the "essence of Christianity," Jesus' discovery and proclamation of the "infinite value of the human soul." Man's value is derived from the fact that he was created by God, who continues to care about him. Bultmann, on the other hand, insists that man has value only when he decides for God in the "crisis of decision." Bultmann's position corresponds to a characteristic Lutheran tendency to regard "faith" as the greatest of works, as, indeed, the sole basis for human value in the eyes of God. Harnack and Bultmann are both touching part of the truth. Bultmann is correct in that faith is inextricably correlated to the perception of value. As H. R. Niebuhr has shown, faith is the bond of confidence and loyalty between the self and the object of faith which is, as such, at the same time the source or center of meaning and of value. Harnack did not recognize that the "Fatherhood of God" and the "infinite value of the human soul" are faith statements, not objective truths. Furthermore, man's value is not, from the standpoint of Jesus' own radically monotheistic faith, an "independent" or "infinite" value, but, as Harnack himself seemed to understand when he associated this value with the Fatherhood of God, it is a *relational* value. Man has value in relation to the source of all value, God. He may have, to God, more value than many sparrows or sheep, but he does not have absolute value: e.g., more than *all* sparrows or sheep or other "lesser" forms of being. Schweitzer and H. R. Niebuhr correctly point out that an ethic which is concerned only with man as the locus of all value is, from the standpoint of radical monotheism or reverence for life, a tribalistic or henotheistic ethic. Furthermore, man does not have absolute value in relation either to other men or to God, who alone is absolutely "good." The neighbor whom I encounter in this particular situation does not have absolute value over against other neighbors in the present or other situations.[7] But Bultmann is wrong in restricting value to those who decide correctly in the "Now" of decision. The God of radical monotheistic faith—as such was incarnate both in the men of faith in ancient Israel and in Jesus of Nazareth—is the universal Creator, Sovereign, and Redeemer, not a tribal god who is concerned only for men of the tribe of faith. The Synoptic Jesus admonished his followers to be concerned not only for one another, as in the case of the Johannine Jesus' restrictive "love of the brethren"—the love of fellow clansmen practiced by the Gentiles—but to love all men, including their enemies and persecutors, after the pattern of God's love which is not reserved for the "good" and "just," but also bestowed on the "evil and unjust."[8]

The recognition in faith that all men (indeed, all existent beings) have value in relation to God is an ever-relevant corrective against the ever-present tendency on the part of men to find relatively greater—and even exclusive—value in those who in nation, race, culture, time, class, sex, or thought are so blessed as to resemble themselves most closely. To such faith there is no longer any distinction in value between "chosen people" and "barbarians," male and female, East and West, Negroid, Oriental, and Caucasian, Communist and capitalist, believer and "infidel."

Schweitzer's several theories by way of explaining Jesus' significance for us are of interest, but the two most important are his conception of the significance of Jesus' will for "our" will, and his characterization of Jesus' ethic as an ethic of "self-devotion to others." The first expresses the sense of authority that Schweitzer found in the person as well as the words of Jesus. It is not just because the sayings of Jesus were imaginatively or "beautifully" spoken and written that they have had meaning in later times. These sayings express the understanding of a particular authoritative and perceptive person (whom the Christian church, for want of a better title, has designated "the Christ") with respect to the nature and demand or will of God. That person took God so seriously as to undertake in his life and message to exemplify and inform his contemporaries as to His will, and of their ultimate situation in relation to God. The person as well as the message of Jesus present the claim of God upon man. God not only values all being, he also wills that it be ordered in such a way as to realize the well-being of all the particular beings in the realm of being.[9] The message of Jesus has to do not only with values but with the will of the Valuer. The will of Jesus, his will to will the will of God, is both norm and authority for the wills of his followers. Schweitzer did not spell out the content of Jesus' will. He did describe the will of God as his "will of love," which Jesus taught that men were to "help carry out in this world." In his later descriptions of Jesus' ethics as the "ethics of love" or "self-devotion to others," Schweitzer made it clear what he understood the content of Jesus' will to be: that his followers love, i.e., be devoted to the well-being of others.

Ethics may be described as the aspect of a person's faith in the object of faith as center of value, in which the person commits or devotes himself to that object as the cause which he desires and wills to serve. When the object of faith is God, the center of value for all that is, ethics, as devotion to God, entails devotion to the concrete manifestations of being which one encounters, thus other human beings (and nonhuman beings as well). Schweitzer did not indicate explicitly that devotion to God is the ground of the self's devotion to others, but this understanding seems implicit in his references to God's will of love. In any case, the conception of Jesus' ethics as the ethics of self-devotion to others illumines the relational character of love as concern for others, expressed in appropriate action with respect to their well-being. The relational nature of love has not always been so clearly understood. Though Jesus spoke very little about love or loving, a great many of his sayings and parables have to do with attitudes and actions relating to the well-being of others.

Bultmann's conception of Jesus' (and also Christian) ethics as the ethics of radical obedience contains two focuses. In relation to God, it means complete surrender of my will to God's will. But (as with Schweitzer), what God wills is that I love my neighbor. This does not mean the surrender of the will to arbitrary external authority, as in Orthodox Judaism and Islam. But it does mean obedience to God, not merely going about business as usual, as if ethics were no more than a refinement of man's quest for pleasure. "Which God will you serve, the Lord or Baal?" thundered Elijah at Mt. Carmel. Jesus, who also came to cast fire upon the earth, presented his generation with a similar choice: No one can serve two masters; you cannot serve God and mammon. Baal and mammon represent the gods that men have always served gladly, for these gods—so their adherents suppose—can be made to serve the purposes of their worshipers. Bultmann correctly perceives that in every moral decision it must be decided anew, Do I choose to serve myself, or to serve God and my neighbor? Unless this question is decided, all talk about "values," "rules," "the situation," or even "love" is likely to be no more than a smoke screen behind which we maneuver so as to serve ourselves. "Repentance" or "conversion" has to do with this fundamental moral decision. Jesus summoned his hearers to turn from their self-centered concerns and toward God, to cease taking themselves with absolute seriousness and to begin to take God seriously as the One who has always manifested his sovereignty in nature and soon would assert it in history. Only when faith has turned from the small gods who serve the self to the One whose cause is the whole realm of being can one begin to affirm and serve one's companions in being in the same way that one otherwise affirms and serves one's own well-being. Conversion is that turning of faith from one god to another. With the redirection of faith, there comes a redirection of ethics: from the self-serving ethics of faith as confidence in and loyalty to self, to the neighbor-serving ethics of faith as confidence in and loyalty to God, whose will is love, i.e., whose cause is the well-being of all his children and creatures.

The ethics of radical obedience or conversion involves the recognition and affirmation of value in the neighbor. The neighbor is not loved because one is commanded to love him: I am going to be nice to you because I have to, even though I despise you. Rather, the neighbor is perceived as one whose well-being is important to God, and received, in H. R. Niebuhr's phrase, as a "companion in being," as a member of one's own family in the family of being. Sometimes we love our brothers and sisters because we know we ought to do so. These are moments of obedience. But in those too uncommon moments when we respond to our brother or sister in being as one whose life and joy or sorrow touch our own, as one whom, in fact, we do love, we experience the meaning of *radical* obedience.

Other terms have also been used to describe this difference: the ethics of grace or "the higher righteousness," as against law; or of inwardness or disposition, as against outward act; or of spirit, against flesh; or of the "new being" or "new creation." Like the phrase "radical obedience," all these terms unfortunately point to the condition of the self, rather than to the relationship between the self and the neighbor. For this reason, the term "love" or some other relational category, such as "self-devotion to others," is necessary in order to complete the meaning. Otherwise, the perversion of ethics lies at hand in the form of pretension to "virtue." Paul's unruly Corinthians prided themselves on their "spirituality," instead of concerning themselves with the well-being of the weaker brethren and the edification and upbuilding of the church. Likewise, the saints of all ages have stood on precarious ground when they began to think of their saintliness, humility, or even faith, hope, and love as virtues or "qualities" they meritoriously possessed, rather than of the needs and well-being of others.

C. H. Dodd's contribution has already been noted: the manner in which Jesus' sayings and parables in fact (even if not so intended) appeal to our imagination, as we find ourselves in situations analogous to those of his hearers or of the persons in his stories. There is always some degree of analogy in any situation wherever two (or more) persons come together, for in any situation, there is the possibility of discovering the other as neighbor and of being neighbor to the other, and there is always the temptation to treat the neighbor as if he were someone else's brother, as if he were not even one of the least of Jesus' brethren, and to pass by on the other side of the road.

The Meaning of Love as a Relational Term

The relevance of Jesus and his ethics is not confined, then, to the "commandment" or "principle" of love. Nevertheless, love is certainly a central category, even when expressed in other terms, such as "self-devotion to others," "the higher righteousness," or "radical obedience." It is important to try to understand the meaning of love. Love is often construed as a subjective phenomenon, as feeling of some sort. Love can appear in sentimentality or romanticism as affection, or in eroticism as desire or lust. Love is also often represented objectively, as a hypostasis or predicate, for instance, by Fletcher. Understood relationally, love has both subjective and objective elements.

Love involves the subject or self, both as one knows oneself to be under requirement, and as one who experiences concern for the other person. Love is not simply obedience to requirement: in love as *radical* obedience, one *desires* the well-being of the other person, and at the same time knows that this is what God desires, wills, and requires. Thus, love includes but is not confined to the performance of acts or "doing good." It also includes affection or "goodwill." There is such a thing as loveless love. The performance of "good deeds" or "acts of charity" may be without love, i.e., without genuine desire for the good of the other person. Paternalistic love is likely to suffer from this defect. Genuine love includes compassion, suffering with the neighbor in his distress, and rejoicing in his joy. It includes, as Buber has pointed out so effectively against Heidegger, the fulfillment of one's own being in the relationship of being with the neighbor, the other self, the thou.[10] Love includes liking, enjoying being together with one's neighbor. But already, it is clear that love is not subjective feeling alone; rather, it is to be found in the relationship of the self with other selves.

The objective aspect of love is not love itself, but the objective well-being of the other person, or of the totality of persons involved in "the situation." The peril of subjective love, whether as sentimentality, eroticism, or paternalism, is that the objective (as well as subjective) well-being of the other person is ignored. The sentimentalist indulges in the enjoyment of his feelings, but does not translate these into actions beneficial to his companions in being. The "playboy" seeks the satisfaction of his own erotic desires, but regards his partner of the moment as "disposable."[11] The paternalist also ignores the objective needs of his beneficiaries: because he thinks he knows already what is good for them, he does not bother to listen to them or otherwise exert himself to discover their actual situation. He quiets any suspicion he may have that something more or different may be needed with the pleasant feeling that he has, after all, done something good. In exchange, he expects gratitude, a clue to the self-serving function of his ethics. Love cannot be guided entirely by the subjectivity of the other person however. Permissiveness results —if not from indifference or even hostility to the other person —from the supposition that what the other person *wants* is *good for* him. Such, of course, is not always the case. Love understood as a relational category, however, is neither paternalistic nor permissive: it means devotion to the other person in both attitude and action. Love, understood relationally, is both subjective and objective. Love is subjective in that it involves the subject's concern or desire, but this desire relates to the objective well-being of the other person, and is expressed concretely in appropriate action. But what is appropriate? To answer that question, it is necessary to examine the meaning of "the situation."

THE NATURE AND DIMENSION OF "THE SITUATION"

Bultmann describes the situation of encounter and moral decision as taking place in "empty space." Here, without reference to any "standard," "past experience," or "rational deductions" one will, if obedient to God, recognize the "one command" that is "the divine requirement," and thereby know what to do.[12] Bultmann seems to understand, however, that in every situation, what God requires is "radical obedience," i.e., love of neighbor. Fletcher, who also supposes that in every situation there is *one* "right" or "good" thing to do, is more explicit as to the centrality of love: "Love decides there and then."[13] His description of the functioning of love in the situation is not particularly edifying, however, because of his objectification of love as "good in and of itself." In Fletcher's confused account of the situation, love serves love: anything is right "if in *this* circumstance love gains the balance" or love is served.[14] What he means, of course, or should mean, is that love exists relationally in the situation as persons affirm and serve the well-being of other persons. Bishop Robinson is clearer on this point than Fletcher. Love is not "the highest good." Neither, however, are the neighbor's *needs*.[15] Rather, the neighbor himself, thus his well-being, is the focus of concern. Love, then, is not an entity, but functions in the situation, perhaps along with other related relational values, such as humility, forgiveness, prudence (or good sense), justice, and courage, all of which have to do with one's relationship with the other persons involved. Courage, for instance, means the willingness to risk one's own well-being for the sake of the neighbor's.

But how is the situation to be defined? Bultmann and Fletcher both tend to view each situation as discrete in time: past and future are unimportant; now alone matters. Paul Ramsey correctly recognizes that the past is part of the situation after all. One brings to the situation certain "summary rules" or "summary principles," i.e., what Bishop Robinson calls "the cumulative experience of one's own and other people's obedience."[16] The past of the other person or persons is also a part of the situation. The physician reviews the medical history as well as the present symptoms of his patient. The past emotional, spiritual, and moral histories of persons are ingredients in the situation. One can respond with understanding and effectiveness to the individual and collective Negro reactions of alienation and frustration that appear in the summer riots only when their past, and the past of their ancestors, is recognized for what it was: slavery, repression, brutality, segregation, and exploitation at the hands of whites, whose own guilty past is also an ingredient in the present. Thus humility and contrition are relevant modes of response, as well as love, forgiveness, and justice.

The situation also extends into the future. What we do now not only will have consequences for ourselves but for others, some of whom do not appear when we take only a narrow view of the situation. The unwanted child of pleasure-seeking lovers (whether married or not) suffers though he was not yet present in the earlier now of decision. The costs of war include not only the soldiers and civilians killed and bereaved but the loss of infinite human lives not yet conceived, as France and Britain know too well. The consequences for the persons in the situation also extend indeterminately into the future. Emotional and physical breakdown may result in the future from doing what now seems "right," for instance, when the college girl who thought that "this" was real love discovers that her erstwhile sexual partner no longer cares for her (if he ever did), or when the boy who experimented with psychedelic drugs finds that he cannot return from the realm of confusion. The situation extends backward and forward in time.

It also extends laterally into space. In nearly every situation there are more than two people. Ramsey proposes that by Jesus' eschatological outlook, all other neighbors "except the one actually present were apocalyptically removed from view and taken care of by God." But as he points out, "There is no such situation in a non-apocalyptic world."[17] Even a literalistic reading of Jesus' radical sayings does not support Ramsey's interpretation. Jesus did not say, for example, "Give everything you have to the first man who wants to borrow from you," or "When you give a feast, invite one poor, maimed, lame, and blind man." Jesus evidently expected his disciples to respond helpfully to more than one neighbor. Ramsey is correct, however, in pointing out the tendency on the part of latter-day disciples to hide their own security and well-being behind a cloak of multiple and conflicting neighbor claims. The fact is, as Ramsey points out, whether Jesus recognized it or not, in our world, we find a number of neighbors in the situation.

Fletcher generally tries to reduce the number of persons involved in the situation to the fewest possible. Thus, in various examples, he glibly states that under certain circumstances "even killing 'innocent' people might be right."[18] It might be less evil than the suffering and death of a still greater number of people, but it can hardly be "right." It would not be plausible to argue that it is right or good for those who are killed! In order to avoid recognizing the ambiguous and tragic character of many a situation, Fletcher prefers to draw a gerrymandered border around it, thus excluding the victims of one's "right" act from consideration, and thus also sparing the "righteous" any sense of guilt.[19] As Schweitzer points out in his chapter on the ethics of reverence for life, a sense of guilt serves an essential purpose, in that it makes one aware of the evil in the situation and keeps one alert to the possibilities of reducing that evil.[20] Otherwise, one can accept tragic consequences (especially for others) with complacency. The consolation that one has done the "right" thing when one has acted harmfully toward even one person in order to help others is a dangerous illusion. As Schweitzer says in the sentence Fletcher himself twice quotes: "The good conscience is an invention of the devil."[21]

The "others" cannot be excluded from the situation by waving a wand. It is likely to include, for instance, not only the boy and the girl who now wish to make each other (and themselves) happy, but also a parent or two who may suffer deep anguish when they learn of their child's "innocent" frolic. Those who take psychedelic drugs without, apparently, damaging themselves or their posterity nevertheless may by their example contribute to the downfall of "weaker brethren." Obviously, the casualty statistics from Vietnam only begin to measure the losses incurred by wives (and some husbands), children, parents, brothers, sisters, and loved ones on both (or all) "sides" of the conflict. It is, in fact, nearly impossible to circumscribe most situations. In many areas of life now the situation is worldwide. It is in our power to destroy the lives of millions of humans and other creatures. It is in our power to provide medicine, technological aid, jobs, and food to millions of diseased, unemployed, and hungry people.

Because there are so many others whose existence complicates the situation, it is tempting to retreat behind intuition or magic: to suppose, with Bultmann and Fletcher, that God, the situation, or love will tell us what to do. The difficulty with this approach is that it does not take the actual situation seriously enough. If the situation, or, more precisely, the combination or structure of factors operating helpfully and harmfully upon the persons in the situation is decisive, there is then a moral responsibility to gain what knowledge one can about the situation. The morally responsible person cannot decide on the basis of intuition or in empty space. He must seek to know the facts of the situation as these affect persons. He will need to learn what he can from history, sociology, psychology, politics, technology, and all other areas of understanding that may have some bearing on the well-being of the persons involved. He may even have to become involved in the situation himself, or recognize that he is already involved in it! When the situation is taken seriously, situation ethics becomes social ethics.

Eschatology as a Dimension of the Situation

Were the Kingdom of God now present, there would be no need for ethics or teachers of ethics, for then, says the prophet Jeremiah, in the name of the Lord:

I will put my law within them,
And I will write it upon their hearts;
and I will be their God,
and they shall be my people.
And no longer shall each man teach his neighbor and each his brother,
saying, "Know the LORD,"
for they shall all know me,
from the least of them to the greatest,
says the LORD.[22]

Those writers who, following Paul, describe the Christian life as a "new creation," or a life in grace, in Christ, or in the Spirit, are testifying to the experience of forgiveness or reconciliation which is based, in the Christian tradition, upon the ministry, suffering, death, and resurrection of Jesus. This past event—though not the arrival of the Kingdom of God—is a decisive part of the present situation. The Christian experiences himself, as Bultmann puts it, as one who has been freed from himself, so that he can be unreservedly for his neighbor.[23] This experience may be related to the experience of conversion or repentance—turning from self to God and neighbor—which Jesus evidently considered to be an existential possibility and necessity for his hearers who wished to enter the Kingdom of God when it came. Jesus apparently understood that God would accept the repentant sinner (with "joy," in fact)[24] apart from the necessity of his own death,[25] belief in himself as the Christ, participation in the sacraments or other later Christian doctrines and institutions.

The future advent of the Kingdom was clearly a matter of consequence to Jesus. Its coming, though still future, was a decisive factor in the present situation. Soon it would be too late to repent. Those found unprepared—having exploited their fellows, or failed to respond to them in times of distress, in short, those who were indifferent to God and neighbor—would be judged adversely. God, himself, would take charge of history, possibly through the Son of Man or Messiah; in any case, it would be God, no longer Satan, the demons, and the "rulers of this age" who ruled the earth. The message that God's Kingdom was coming was "good news" to those who had been faithful to him, who had sought righteousness and reconciliation, and had been humble and pure of heart even at the cost of persecution and physical privation, for they would inherit the Kingdom on earth. It is unlikely that Jesus understood this gospel as "myth." Yet even if we do so regard it, its meaning for us is not thereby dissipated.

There are at least two features of the eschatological hope that are relevant for our moral situations. As in the case of Jesus' hearers, so for us also, time is short. Not only does our own life come to an end soon—we know not when, but surely within the span of a normal lifetime—but also the lifetime of others is similarly limited. We do not have an infinity of time in which to respond to our neighbor who now needs our help. He may not be there tomorrow. Or perhaps we will not be. Many encounters or situations are highly limited in time, at least so far as the time when we can act responsibly is concerned. We and those who come after us will have to live (or suffer) for generations with the consequences of our actions or failures to act now, but we do not have forever in which to act. It is now too late already, for instance, to avert the scar of racial hatred in our country. We have tried to heal the wounds of our people lightly by saying "peace, peace" when there was no peace. When we became aware in earlier decades that educational and job opportunities, housing and justice, were manifestly unequally apportioned between races, we could have acted with contrition and concern to atone for the sins of the fathers (and some of our own complicity). Our response, such as it was, came in the form of tokenism. What is done now is not likely to be done out of contrition, but because the self-interest of the white majority and the national interest are in jeopardy. By the time our nation officially recognizes the existence of Communist China, it will be too late to do so with good grace in quest of a basis of coexistence if not reconciliation. We will be forced to it by Chinese power (as China was forced to recognize the existence of the West somewhat over a century ago). By then it may be too late for coexistence. In history, a people normally pay for the sins of the past: the whirlwind will be reaped. Tomorrow it may be too late to make and effect the moral decision that is called for today. Some damage cannot be undone. The Negro children who, since 1954, have continued to be the recipients of a separate but unequal education have been permanently damaged. The victims of war in Vietnam have already paid for our decisions, and more will pay tomorrow for our decisions and indecisions of yesterday and today. All ethics are interim ethics.

Eschatology is relevant to the contemporary moral life in yet another way: as hope. God is no *deus ex machina* who can be depended upon to deliver his chosen people from catastrophe in the last act. Eschatology includes judgment, and those who imagine themselves heirs to the promise do well to ponder Amos' declaration:

> You only have I known
> of all the families of the earth;
> therefore I will punish you
> for all your iniquities.
> (Amos 3:2.)

It may be that America and Western civilization, as we have known them, must go under. And yet, this is not "the end" if God is the one who is at work in and against history to bring his purposes to fulfillment. We no longer look for the Kingdom of God to appear in history as the end result of natural evolution or of moral effort. If history is to be redeemed, it will be as in the case of our own little individual histories: a miracle of his grace.

We do not spend our time profitably in trying to visualize the architecture and city plan for the "new Jerusalem." As with all symbols of the ultimate, our images and formulas are inevitably crude and pretentious if not idolatrous. Yet the understanding that God will ultimately reveal and actualize his Lordship over history, however expressed symbolically, means that the present historical situation has meaning. Historical, material existence is not viewed as a mistake, or as a consequence of a "fall" from pure spirituality. Nor is salvation perceived in terms of immortal, ethereal life in a realm beyond space and time. Space and time are sanctified by the prospect of God's redeeming activity in space and time. The ambiguities of history will be resolved. The principalities and powers, including our own will to power, will be judged. The cruelties and pretensions of our past and present will be recognized as such. In redemption there will be contrition and judgment:

> A new heart I will give you,
> and a new spirit I will put within you;
> and I will take out of your flesh the heart of stone
> and give you a heart of flesh.
> . . . .
> You shall dwell in the land which I gave to your fathers;
> and you shall be my people, and I will be your God.
> . . . .
> Then you will remember your evil ways,
> and your deeds that were not good;
> and you will loathe yourselves for your iniquities
> and your abominable deeds.[26]

Perhaps the most terrible kind of judgment is that which comes with the recognition of what we have done. There is nothing arbitrary or external about that judgment. In any case, the expectation of judgment, as this may be experienced in, and ultimately at the end of, our individual and collective histories, gives meaning to the present situation in which we encounter concretely our various neighbors. We readily come under the illusion that what we do as individuals or as a people makes no difference: there seems to be so little that we can do, so why bother? We cannot save mankind, so why should we worry about those few whom we can help? The prospect of judgment gives expression to the realization that our actions and inactions are of ultimate importance, for by them we sustain or fail to sustain our fellow beings, each of whom is important to the Ultimate Source of being, who wills the being and well-being of each.

The prospect of salvation does not render less serious our moral situation. But it gives the hope that God can overrule our at best partly adequate, but often guilty responses, and accomplish his purposes for men and all of creation despite, as well as with, our help. The prospect of forgiveness makes it possible for us to acknowledge our guilt and begin, even now, in our continuing historical existence to experience that grace or forgiveness which liberates us from bondage not only to our sins but to our illusions of virtue. Thereby we begin to be liberated for our neighbors.

Notes

Chapter I. The Liberal Version of the Teaching of Jesus—*Adolf von Harnack*

1. *What Is Christianity?* tr. by T. B. Saunders (Harper & Brothers, 1957), p. 114. Reprinted with the permission of Harper Torchbooks, Harper & Row, Publishers, Inc. Harnack still clung, wistfully, to this hope as late as 1917: see his sermon "Vom Reiche Gottes," in *Erforschtes und Erlebtes* (Giessen: Alfred Töpelmann, 1923), pp. 383 f., where he concedes that this war-torn world seems far removed from the Kingdom of God, but urges still that God's "Kingdom is established amongst us, and is gaining ground."

2. Ernst Käsemann, James M. Robinson, *et al.* See also the current reissues of various classic "lives of Jesus," and the interest in Jesus on the part of some of the "death of God" and other "new" theologians.

3. Whether dogmas of moral theology, as in the case of the proponents of "situation ethics," the dogmas of traditional faith, as with Bishops Robinson and Pike, or the dogmas of cultural and social mythology, e.g., Peter Berger and Harvey Cox. The decline of interest in Barth and his dogmatics is also a sign of the times.

4. *What Is Christianity?* (hereafter cited as *What?*), with an Introduction by Rudolf Bultmann; *Outlines of the History of Dogma* (hereafter cited as *Outlines*), tr. by E. K. Mitchell (Beacon Press, Inc., 1957), with an Introduction by Philip Rieff; *History of Dogma* (hereafter cited as *History*), Vols. I–VII, tr. by N. Buchanan (Dover Publications, Inc., 1961); and *The Mission and Expansion of Christianity in the First Three Centuries* (hereafter cited as *Mission*), tr. by J.

Moffatt (Harper & Row, Publishers, Inc., 1961), with an Introduction by Jaroslav Pelikan.

5. *Das Wesen des Christentums* (Leipzig: J. C. Hinrichs'sche Buchhandlung, 1900); English trans., *What Is Christianity?*

6. Paul Tillich, *Theology of Culture* (Oxford University Press, Inc., 1964), pp. 161 f.

7. E.g., *What?* p. 157: "His death had the value of an expiatory sacrifice"; and p. 38: "He lived in the continual consciousness of God's presence." Harnack publicly acknowledged that these two had correctly grasped the true nature of religion and the gospel: see *Thoughts on the Present Position of Protestantism,* tr. by T. B. Saunders (London: Adam and Charles Black, Ltd., 1899), pp. 26, 56. Cf. *A Scholar's Testament,* tr. by O. Wyon (London: Ivor Nicholson & Watson, Ltd., 1933), p. 119.

8. E.g., *What?* p. 6: "In dealing with religion, is it not after all with the Christian religion alone that we have to do? Other religions no longer stir the depths of our hearts." See also pp. 41, 269 ff., 300.

9. In this connection, see Dietrich Bonhoeffer, "Gedächtnisrede auf Adolf v. Harnack" (June 15, 1930), in *Ausgewählte Reden und Aufsätze,* ed. by Agnes von Zahn-Harnack and Axel von Harnack (Berlin: de Gruyter, 1951), pp. 210 f.

10. *What?* p. 130.

11. *History,* I, p. 77.

12. *What?* p. 130.

13. *Ibid.,* p. 14.

14. See *History,* I, pp. 16–23.

15. *What?* p. 30.

16. "Vorfragen, die Glaubwürdigkeit der evangelischen Geschichte betreffend" (1904), in *Aus Wissenschaft und Leben* (Giessen: A. Töpelmann, 1911), Vol. II, pp. 186 ff.

17. By 1900, Harnack had read Martin Kähler's now famous book regarding this problem, *The So-called Historical Jesus and the Historical, Biblical Christ* (Leipzig: A. Deichert, 1896; English trans. by C. E. Braaten, Fortress Press, 1964), cited in *History,* I, p. 72.

18. *What?* p. 31.

19. *The Sayings of Jesus, The Second Source of St. Matthew and St. Luke* (hereafter cited as *Sayings*), tr. by J. R. Wilkinson, New Testament Studies, Vol. II (London: Williams & Norgate, 1908), p. 250; see also p. 231.

20. *Luke the Physician,* New Testament Studies, Vol. I (London: Williams & Norgate, 1907), pp. 160 ff.

21. *Sayings,* p. 249.

22. "Vorfragen," p. 210; see also *Luke the Physician.*

23. *Luke the Physician,* pp. 167 ff.

24. *Sayings,* p. 209: "Judged in detail and as a whole, all that is presented as teaching of our Lord in the Sermon on the Mount bears the stamp of unalloyed genuineness."

25. *History,* pp. 64n3, 65n2.

26. *What?* p. x.

27. Johannes Weiss, *Die Predigt Jesu vom Reiche Gottes* (Göttingen: Vandenhoeck & Ruprecht, 1892).

28. *History,* I, p. 62n1.

29. *What?* p. 53.

30. *Das Wesen des Christentums* (Stuttgart: Ehrenfried Klotz Verlag, 1950), Preface to the 10th edition (1903), p. xix.

31. *History,* I, p. 58; cf. *What?* p. 53.

32. *History,* I, pp. 58 ff.; see also *Outlines,* p. 15.

33. *Outlines,* p. 15; see also *What?* p. 62.

34. *History,* I, p. 62.

35. *What?* p. 214.

36. *Ibid.,* p. 56; see also p. 77.

37. *What?* pp. 61 f. Harnack hinged his whole contention that Jesus understood the Kingdom to be present in the hearts of men on Luke 17:21 (p. 54). It is quite unlikely, however, that this verse contains such a meaning. See the writer's article on this verse in the *Journal of the American Academy of Religion,* Vol. XXXV (1967), pp. 379–384.

38. Walter Rauschenbusch, *A Theology for the Social Gospel* (The Macmillan Company, 1917; Abingdon Press reprint, n.d.), p. 145.

39. "Vom Reiche Gottes," p. 389.

40. *Outlines,* p. 15.

41. *What?* pp. 53 f. See also *History,* I, p. 58: "We are following . . . the requirement of the thing itself, when, in the presentation of the Gospel, we place in the foreground, not that which unites it with the contemporary disposition of Judaism, but that which raises it above it."

42. *History,* I, p. 58.

43. *What?* p. 56.

44. *History,* I, p. 66.

45. *What?* pp. 54 f.

46. *Ibid.,* pp. 13 f., 191; *History,* I, p. 74.

47. *What?* pp. 8, 14, 143, 184, 205, 275; *History,* I, p. 61; *Outlines,* p. 10.

48. *Das Wesen,* p. xix; *What?* p. 7.

49. *History,* p. 75; *Das Wesen,* pp. xvii, xix, xxii; *What?* pp. 6 f., 9.

50. *What?* p. 9. The title of the English translation is derived from this question.

51. *What?* p. 11; *Outlines,* p. 12. Harnack frequently referred to Jesus as "the founder" of Christianity. He even states on one occasion that Jesus "himself" was "convinced" that the religion which he and the apostles "were planting would in the ages to come have a greater destiny and a deeper meaning" (*What?* p. 11), even though he admits elsewhere that "Jesus seems to have announced . . . [his own] speedy return a short time before his death" (*History,* I, p. 66). Here is another ambiguity (or contradiction) in Harnack's position.

52. *What?* pp. 55, 180, 190 f.; *History,* I, p. 75.

53. *What?* p. 269, italics added. See also p. 272: "What . . . was involved was a *renewal* of religion; . . . a return to Christianity as it originally was"; and p. 284: "The Gospel was in reality re-won." See also *History,* VII, pp. 227 f.

54. *Outlines,* p. 4; *What?* pp. 299 f.

55. *What?* pp. 289 ff.; see also *History,* VII, esp. pp. 230 ff.

56. *History,* I, p. 6.

57. *Ibid.,* p. 75. See also *What?* p. 14: "Getting rid of formulas, correcting expectations, . . . is a process to which there is no end." He goes on to add, however, that his "survey embraces the whole course as well as the inception." Does this mean that the "process" has now come to an end after all?

58. *What?* p. 18.

59. *Ibid.,* pp. 48, 272; *Outlines,* p. 550.

60. *History,* I, pp. 65 f.

61. See, esp., Albert Schweitzer, *The Quest of the Historical Jesus* (The Macmillan Company, 1950), Ch. XIX.

62. *What?* p. 191.

63. *History,* I, pp. 74 f.

64. *Ibid.,* p. 22.

65. *Ibid.* If his own appreciation of the importance of dogma as

"faith seeking understanding" was underdeveloped, Harnack was at least alert to the danger with respect to religious forms or symbols: "The value of that to which they minister is insensibly transferred to them" (*What?* p. 181; see also pp. 184, 211 f.). Paul Tillich and H. R. Niebuhr were also particularly concerned about the fact that symbols become "idols" when granted the sanctity of the Ultimate in which they participate.

66. *What?* pp. 218, 262.

67. *Ibid.*, pp. 266 f., 269, 299.

68. *What?* pp. 15, 298. Note Harnack's tendency to hypostatize "the Gospel." Later, Bultmann would hypostatize "the Kerygma."

69. E.g., *What?* p. 180: "Without doing violence to the inner and essential features of the Gospel . . . Paul transformed it into the universal religion." It may be significant that Harnack devotes little space to Paul and offers no thoroughgoing discussion of his beliefs, not even in his study of *The Mission and Expansion of Christianity*, or in his *History of Dogma*.

70. See, for example, his summaries of early Christian faith and ethics in *What?* p. 189, and *Mission*, pp. 147 ff.

71. *What?* pp. 13 f.

72. E.g., *ibid.*, pp. 73 f., where Harnack attributes his own four categories concerning "the higher righteousness" to Jesus himself. W. Sanday commented tersely, but with less than full justice, that by "Gospel," Harnack meant "Harnack's version of the leading points in Christ's teaching" (*An Examination of Harnack's 'What Is Christianity?'* [London: Longmans, Green & Co., Ltd., 1901], p. 14). *What?* pp. 51, 77: these three categories provide his outline for pp. 52–78.

73. *What?* p. 51.

74. *Ibid.*, also pp. 62, 68, 70, 77.

75. *Ibid.*, p. 77. Note Harnack's reductionist and individualistic tendencies here: the Kingdom is not seen as a community, and there is no mention in this ultimate synthesis of "the higher righteousness showing itself in love."

76. *History*, I, p. 59; also *Outlines*, p. 16.

77. *Thoughts on the Present Position*, p. 55.

78. *What?* pp. 56, 142, 263.

79. *Ibid.*, p. 214, also pp. 143 f.

80. *Ibid.*, p. 70.

81. *Ibid.*, pp. 67 f., 99–101; cf. p. 189.

82. *History,* I, p. 70, italics added; see also *What?* pp. 99 f.
83. *What?* pp. 70 ff., 77.
84. *Ibid.,* pp. 72 f.; see also "Das Urchristentum und die socialen Fragen" (1908) in *Aus Wiss. u. Leben,* II, pp. 268–271; *What?* pp. 71 f.
85. *Monasticism, Its Ideals and History,* tr. by E. E. Kellett and F. H. Marseille (London: Williams & Norgate, 1913), p. 17.
86. *What?* pp. 48, 84, 146, 180, 299.
87. *Ibid.,* pp. 96, 125; *History,* I, pp. 60, 78; *Sayings,* pp. 231, 251 f.
88. *What?* p. 111; cf. *History,* I, p. 62n1.
89. Sanday, *op. cit.,* p. 7.
90. The writings of E. F. Scott, B. H. Branscomb, A. C. Knudson, and L. H. Marshall in varying degrees exemplify this conception.
91. *What?* pp. 10, 48 f., 51.
92. *Ibid.,* p. 144.
93. *Ibid.,* p. 299.
94. *Ibid.,* p. 48. Cf. p. 51: "He himself stands behind everything that he said."
95. *Outlines,* pp. 10 f. Cf. *History,* I, pp. 70 f.: "He himself . . . is Christianity. . . . We cannot therefore state the 'doctrine' of Jesus; for it appears as a supramundane life which must be felt in the person of Jesus."
96. *History,* I, p. 72.
97. *What?* pp. 60, 146.
98. *Ibid.,* p. 128. Notice here, again, the reductionist "nothing but." Harnack similarly describes the prophetic work of Jesus in his essay, "Christus als Erlöser" (1899), in *Ausgewählte Reden und Aufsätze,* pp. 144 f.: Jesus "brought the perfect knowledge of God."
99. *History,* I, p. 65n3.
100. *What?* p. 51.
101. "Eröffnungsrede beim 21. Evangelisch-Sozialen Kongress" (1910), in *Aus Wiss. u. Leben,* I, p. 185.
102. See the writer's article "Interim Ethics," in *Theology and Life,* Vol. IX (1966), esp. pp. 224–228.
103. *What?* p. 84, 146; *Monasticism,* p. 17.
104. *What?* p. 87.
105. *Ibid.,* p. 8; see also pp. 17, 115, 121, 149; "Christus als Erlöser," p. 138; and "Was verdankt unsere Kultur den Kirchenvätern" (1910), in *Aus Wiss. u. Leben,* II, p. 4.
106. *What?* p. 17; see also *History,* I, pp. 59, 61.

107. *What?* p. 130. See also *History,* I, p. 43: "The Gospel was a message for humanity even when there was no break with Judaism."

108. *What?* p. 180; *Mission,* p. 45. See also p. 36: "He [Jesus] preached only to Jews."

109. *History,* I, p. 58; *Mission,* p. 16.

110. *Mission,* pp. 36 f.

111. *Ibid.,* p. 43. Harnack did not explain how Jesus' death was to bring about that result. Like the writers of the "liberal lives," Harnack had no way of accounting for Jesus' resolve to meet his death in Jerusalem. It did not occur to them that this momentous decision could have had any connection with his eschatological beliefs, since they supposed that Jesus himself did not take such beliefs seriously.

112. *What?* p. 149.

113. *Ibid.,* see also pp. 14, 275.

114. *Ibid.,* pp. 299 f. Here it is not quite clear whether Harnack meant the "principles of the Reformation" or "the religion of the Gospel." It is to be recalled that Harnack viewed the Reformation as the original gospel rewon; the two, therefore, for him were ultimately the same. See also p. 85, where he implies that a person should feel "compelled to apply these sayings of the Gospel to himself."

115. *What?* pp. 146, 301.

116. *Ibid.,* p. 84.

117. "Eröffnungsrede," p. 187. He speaks here, however, of the problem of sex and marriage, rather than of economic or political decisions. See also *What?* p. 101: "The Gospel is a social message, solemn and over-powering in its force."

118. *What?* pp. 97 f.; see also "The Evangelical Social Mission in the Light of the History of the Church" (1896), in Wilhelm Hermann and Adolf von Harnack, *Essays on the Social Gospel,* tr. by G. M. Craik (London: Williams & Norgate, 1907), pp. 13 f.

119. "Das Urchristentum und die socialen Fragen" (1908) in *Aus Wiss. u. Leben,* II, p. 257.

120. "Evangelical Social Mission," pp. 9 ff.

121. *What?* p. 116; see also p. 111.

122. *Ibid.,* pp. 98 ff.

123. *Ibid.,* p. 116; see also p. 97; and "Evangelical Social Mission," pp. 13 f.

124. "Evangelical Social Mission," p. 15; see also *What?* p. 300.

125. *What?* pp. 100 f.; "Evangelical Social Mission," pp. 3 f.

126. "Evangelical Social Mission," p. 79.

127. *Ibid.,* p. 88.

128. "Vom Reiche Gottes," pp. 389 ff.

129. "Was wir schon gewonnen haben und was wir noch gewinnen müssen" (Sept. 29, 1914), No. 5 in *Deutsche Reden in schwerer Zeit* (Berlin: Carl Heymann, 1914).

130. *Ibid.,* pp. 8 f., 21 f.

131. "September, 1916," in *A Scholar's Testament,* p. 1.

132. *Ibid.,* "Was wir schon gewonnen," p. 14.

133. "14 December, 1919," in *A Scholar's Testament,* p. 208; see also pp. 204 ff., 209.

134. "Evangelical Social Mission," p. 16; see also "Vom Reiche Gottes," pp. 389 f.

135. *What?* pp. 101, 115. And yet Harnack was able to criticize those who think Jesus, "like themselves, a 'Conservative,' who respected all these existing social differences and ordinances as 'divinely ordained' " (p. 90).

136. *What?* pp. 149 f.

137. *Sayings,* p. 251.

138. *History,* I, p. 61; see also *Outlines,* pp. 16 f.; and *What?* p. 143.

139. *What?* p. 143.

CHAPTER II. THE HISTORICAL JESUS VS. MODERN THEOLOGY—*Albert Schweitzer*

1. II Cor. 13:8, cited in *Out of My Life and Thought,* tr. by C. T. Campion (Henry Holt and Co., Inc., 1949), pp. 51, 59; *The Quest of the Historical Jesus,* tr. by W. Montgomery (London: Adam and Charles Black, Ltd., 1954), new Introduction, p. xvi.

2. *Das Messianitäts- und Leidensgeheimnis. Eine Skizze des Lebens Jesu* (Tübingen: J. C. B. Mohr, 1901); English trans. by W. Lowrie, *The Mystery of the Kingdom of God* (The Macmillan Company, 1950).

3. *Die Geschichte der Leben-Jesu-Forschung* (Tübingen: J. C. B. Mohr, 1913). This has not been translated. Its final chapter has been partly translated and published by Walter Lowrie in his Introduction to *The Mystery of the Kingdom of God,* and by Henry Clark, as an Appendix in his book *The Ethical Mysticism of Albert*

Schweitzer (Beacon Press, Inc., 1962). Some of the quotations and page references here will be from one or the other of these translations.

4. *Die psychiatrische Beurteilung Jesu* (Tübingen: J. C. B. Mohr, 1913); English trans. by C. R. Joy, *The Psychiatric Study of Jesus* (Beacon Press, Inc., 1948).

5. *Christianity and the Religions of the World,* tr. by J. Powers (London: George Allen & Unwin, Ltd., 1923).

6. *The Philosophy of Civilization,* tr. by C. T. Campion. Vol. I, *The Decay and the Restoration of Civilization;* Vol. II, *Civilization and Ethics.* References here are to the double-volume edition published by The Macmillan Company, 1960.

7. *The Mysticism of Paul the Apostle,* tr. by W. Montgomery (The Macmillan Company, 1931).

8. See particularly his new Introduction to *The Quest,* published in the 3d ed., London, 1954; and his essay, "The Conception of the Kingdom of God in the Transformation of Eschatology," which appears as an Appendix in E. N. Mozley, *The Theology of Albert Schweitzer* (The Macmillan Company, 1951).

9. *Out,* pp. 46 f.

10. *The Quest,* p. 253.

11. Schweitzer did not claim to be the first to discover the nature and importance of Jesus' eschatological beliefs. In *The Quest* he credits Reimarus with having perceived the matter, if in somewhat distorted form. (Reimarus had supposed that Jesus regarded himself as a *political* messiah.) Schweitzer withholds his highest praise for Johannes Weiss who "first rightly grasped" the nature of Jesus' conception of the Kingdom of God (p. 239).

12. *Mystery,* pp. 53–55.

13. *Ibid.,* p. 56.

14. *Ibid.,* p. 76.

15. *Ibid.,* p. 81.

16. The disciples knew this secret, but only after Peter disclosed it to them at Caesarea Philippi. *Ibid.*

17. *Mysticism,* p. 109.

18. *Ibid.,* pp. 105–108.

19. *Mystery,* p. 137.

20. *Ibid.,* pp. 63–67, 147.

21. *Ibid.,* p. 148; see also "Conception of the Kingdom," pp. 95 f.

22. *Out,* p. 41.

23. *Mysticism,* p. 111.

24. *The Quest,* p. 399; cf. p. 389.

25. See my article "Interim Ethics," pp. 220–233.

26. *Mystery,* p. 174.

27. *The Quest,* p. 403.

28. *Christianity,* pp. 27, 31, 43; *Philosophy,* p. 147; and a recent letter by Schweitzer published in *Rundbrief für den Freundeskreis von Albert Schweitzer* (Jan. 14, 1960), pp. 58 f., quoted in Clark, *op. cit.,* p. 30.

29. *Out,* p. 51.

30. It is often unclear whether Schweitzer means to speak of Jesus' significance for the modern *Christian* or for modern man generally. Perhaps Schweitzer did not intend to differentiate between the two. At any rate, he seemed to feel at home, himself, in both categories.

31. *Geschichte,* pp. 633 f.

32. *Ibid.,* p. 640.

33. *Out,* p. 56. See also *The Quest,* p. 401; and "Conception of the Kingdom," p. 113: "Not for a single moment have I had to struggle for my conviction that in him is the supreme spiritual and religious authority, though his expectation of the speedy advent of a supernatural Kingdom of God was not fulfilled, and we cannot make it our own."

34. *Mysticism,* esp. Ch. XIV. See also *Out,* p. 216: "[Paul] advances thoughts about our relation to Jesus, which ethically and spiritually are final and good for all time."

35. *Out,* pp. 55 f., italics added; see also *Geschichte,* pp. 633 f., quoted above.

36. *Christianity,* p. 26. See also *Geschichte;* English translation in Clark, *op. cit.,* p. 197.

37. *The Quest,* p. 399.

38. *Mystery,* pp. 157–159.

39. *Ibid.,* pp. 158 f.

40. See also *ibid.,* p. 159.

41. Later, in writing on Paul, Schweitzer shows that Paul could not simply take over Jesus' eschatological belief, but he also insists that Paul can be understood correctly only if it is recognized that he *shared* Jesus' basic eschatological viewpoint. E.g., "Conception of the Kingdom," pp. 84 f.

42. *Mystery,* p. 174.

43. *Geschichte,* in Clark, *op. cit.,* p. 202.

44. *Mystery,* pp. 158 f., italics added.
45. *Philosophy,* p. 146.
46. See below, pp. 70 f.
47. *Mystery,* p. 158.
48. *Ibid.,* pp. 158 f., quoted above, also pp. 42 f.
49. *Geschichte,* p. 632; English translation in *Mystery,* p. 9. See also, *The Quest,* p. 399.
50. *The Quest,* p. 250; see also p. 401.
51. He affirms the former in *The Quest,* p. 402, the latter on p. 250. See also *Philosophy,* p. 143.
52. *The Quest* (1954), p. xvi.
53. *Out,* p. 58.
54. *Ibid.*
55. *The Quest,* p. 401.
56. *Ibid.*
57. *Ibid.;* see also *Geschichte,* p. 639.
58. Cf. Henry Clark's critique of Schweitzer's "spiritual Jesus within the historical Jesus": "He uses the spiritual Jesus as the source of inspiration for those very ideals for which the historical Jesus could not serve as authority" (*op. cit.,* p. 81).
59. *Geschichte,* in Clark, *op. cit.,* esp. pp. 196–204.
60. *Geschichte,* p. 636; in *Mystery,* p. 22.
61. *Out,* p. 56.
62. *Geschichte,* p. 634.
63. *Ibid.,* p. 639.
64. See, for example, *Geschichte,* p. 636; in *Mystery,* p. 22.
65. *Geschichte,* in Clark, *op. cit.,* p. 203.
66. *Ibid.,* p. 204.
67. *Mysticism,* p. 379.
68. *Christianity,* p. 27. In this book, Schweitzer never speaks of the will *of Jesus,* but always of the will *of God,* and its specific content, love, e.g., pp. 30 f., 48. Here also, he speaks both of the Spirit of Jesus (p. 85) and of the Spirit of God (p. 31); in both cases, the meaning, evidently, is thought and action done in love. Here, too, he speaks of God's (but not Jesus') revelation of himself "within me," i.e., in individual experience, "as ethical will" or "as Personality" (pp. 32, 76 f.). The vagueness of Schweitzer's Trinitarian (or binitarian) ideas in this book are reminiscent of the apostle Paul's!
69. *Geschichte,* in Clark, *op. cit.,* pp. 203 f.; *Christianity,* p. 28.
70. *Mysticism,* p. 105.

71. *Ibid.,* pp. 106–109, 236 f.
72. *Ibid.,* p. 378.
73. *Ibid.*
74. *Ibid.* See also p. 386: "By his doctrine of the Spirit he [Paul] has himself thrown a bridge from his world-view to ours."
75. *Ibid.,* p. 379; see also *Geschichte,* in Clark, *op. cit.,* pp. 203 f.
76. *Mysticism,* p. 388.
77. He wrote this last chapter dealing with "permanent elements in Paul's mysticism" on shipboard to Africa.
78. *Mysticism,* p. 394; see also pp. 102–110.
79. *Ibid.,* pp. 394 f.
80. *Ibid.,* p. 394; see also p. 396.
81. *Ibid.,* p. 389.
82. *Ibid.,* p. 396.
83. *Out,* pp. 213–216.
84. *Geschichte,* p. 639.
85. *Ibid.,* p. 639; in Clark, *op. cit.,* p. 200.
86. *Ibid.,* pp. 638 f.; in Clark, *op. cit.,* p. 201.
87. *Out,* pp. 57 f.
88. *Philosophy,* pp. 111, 146.
89. *Geschichte,* p. 639; see also pp. 638 f., quoted above; *Mysticism,* pp. 384 f.; and *Out,* p. 54: "The one important thing is that we shall be as thoroughly dominated by the idea of the Kingdom, as Jesus required His followers to be."
90. *The Quest* (1954), p. xv, also p. xvi. See also, *Out,* p. 58: "I was convinced that this liberal Christianity was not reduced to living on an historical illusion, but could equally appeal to the Jesus of history."
91. See "Conception of the Kingdom," p. 110, where he says that the modern Protestant view of the Kingdom is "historically wrong" but "religiously right."
92. *Mysticism,* p. 388.
93. *The Quest* (1954), p. xv; "Conception of the Kingdom," p. 114.
94. "Conception of the Kingdom," pp. 116 f. Schweitzer did not expect that human effort could ever "create the conditions of God's Kingdom in the world." Nevertheless, he urged, "We must indeed labor for its realization" (*ibid.*).
95. *The Quest* (1954), p. xv.
96. *Philosophy,* p. 144.
97. *Ibid.,* pp. 110 f.

98. *Ibid.,* pp. 145 f.

99. *Ibid.,* p. 146.

100. *Ibid.,* pp. 144–146.

101. This confusion is particularly evident on pp. 147 f.

102. *Out,* p. 85.

103. *Ibid.,* pp. 86–89.

104. Schweitzer's reflections on this theme are to be found, principally, in his *Philosophy of Civilization,* Preface, Chs. 22–27, and *passim;* his autobiography, Chs. 13 and 21; and his essay, "The Ethics of Reverence for Life," first published in *Christendom,* I (Winter, 1936), reprinted in Clark, *op. cit.,* pp. 180–194.

105. *Out,* p. 234.

106. *Ibid.,* p. 157.

107. "Reverence for Life," in Clark, *op. cit.,* p. 185.

108. *Philosophy,* p. 287.

109. By this Schweitzer evidently means, in effect, thinking about the existential question, "What is the meaning and purpose of my life?"

110. *Philosophy,* p. 303.

111. *Ibid.,* p. 304.

112. *Ibid.,* p. 305.

113. Paul Tillich, *The Dynamics of Faith* (Harper & Brothers, 1958); H. Richard Niebuhr, *Radical Monotheism and Western Culture* (Harper & Row, Publishers, Inc., 1960).

114. *Philosophy,* pp. 283, 305.

115. It is not always clear what Schweitzer's "center of value" or basic concern is: whether it is "life" (i.e., living beings), more inclusively, "the world," or, less inclusively, "civilization."

116. *Philosophy,* p. 79.

117. *Ibid.,* pp. 80 f.

118. *Ibid.,* p. 340, italics added.

119. *Out,* p. 232.

120. *Ibid.,* esp. Ch. 6; also, "Conception of the Kingdom."

121. *Philosophy,* pp. 144–146, 341.

122. *Christianity and the Religions of the World.*

123. *Out,* p. 58.

124. *Ibid.,* p. 37.

125. *Ibid.,* pp. 58 f.

126. The disappearance of the eschatological world view at any rate makes it necessary to find some other interpretative framework,

world view, philosophy, or mythology expressive of "the religion of Jesus." Schweitzer obviously felt that Jesus' "religion of love" was not identical with "late Jewish" eschatology.

127. *Out,* p. 53.

128. This writer concurs with Krister Stendahl's feeling that the term "late Jewish" is both imprecise and parochial: Christianity did, of course, originate as a Jewish sect in the first century of the common era, but did not represent, historically, the end or culmination of Judaism.

129. *Out,* p. 53.

130. *Ibid.,* p. 54; see also, *Geschichte,* p. 639.

131. *Mystery,* pp. 56 f.

132. *Ibid.,* p. 56.

133. See my article, "Eschatology and Methodology," in *The Journal of Biblical Literature,* Vol. LXXXV (1966), pp. 170–184.

Chapter III. The Message of Jesus—Radical Obedience—*Rudolf Bultmann*

1. *Jesus and the Word,* tr. by L. P. Smith and E. H. Lantero (Charles Scribner's Sons, 1934, 1958), p. 8. Quotations used by permission of Charles Scribner's Sons.

2. *Theology of the New Testament,* tr. by K. Grobel (Charles Scribner's Sons, 1954), Vol. I, p. 32; "The New Approach to the Synoptic Problem" (1926), in *Existence and Faith,* tr. by S. M. Ogden (Meridian Books, Inc., 1960), p. 39; and *The History of the Synoptic Tradition,* tr. by J. March (Harper & Row, Publishers, Inc., 1963), pp. 338–350.

3. *Jesus and the Word,* pp. 12, 126; "New Approach," pp. 38 f.

4. *Jesus and the Word,* p. 13.

5. Bultmann is famous for his announced indifference as to whether the object of his study in *Jesus and the Word* is the historical Jesus or the Synoptic account as it stands. After saying that he believes that Jesus, "according to overwhelming probability," really was the speaker of the sayings in the oldest layer of Synoptic tradition, he adds, "Should it prove otherwise, that does not change in any way what is said in the record" (p. 14). Likewise, while expressing doubt as to the theory that the eschatological sayings were put in Jesus' mouth by the church, he adds: "Yet if it were true, the meaning of the eschatological message would still be fundamentally

the same. . . . The question of how much the historical Jesus and how much other people have contributed to [the content of the Gospels] is of secondary importance" (p. 123).

6. "New Approach," pp. 38 f.

7. *Jesus and the Word,* p. 126.

8. *Ibid.,* pp. 24 f.; *Primitive Christianity in Its Contemporary Setting,* tr. by R. H. Fuller (Meridian Books, Inc., 1956), pp. 75 f.; *Theology,* I, p. 27.

9. *Jesus and the Word,* pp. 57 f.

10. Recently Bultmann has denied that Jesus appeared as a rabbi; rather, he appeared "as a prophet with an eschatological message, though he may also have made use of the doctrine and forms of rabbinic teaching" ("The Primitive Christian Kerygma and the Historical Jesus," in Carl Braaten and Roy Harrisville [trs. and eds.], *The Historical Jesus and the Kerygmatic Christ* [Abingdon Press, 1964], p. 27).

11. *Theology,* I, p. 10; *Jesus and the Word,* p. 28.

12. Bultmann does not explain the existential significance of demon possession or Jesus' cures of those so afflicted. He either speaks of them as here, in matter-of-fact terms, or, as the Fourth Gospel, which he cites as warrant for the procedure of "demythologizing" eschatology, he *eliminates* the "myth" of demons and demon possession *tacitly.*

13. *Jesus and the Word,* p. 108; "Jesus and Paul" (1936), in *Existence and Faith,* p. 193.

14. *Primitive Christianity,* p. 76; *Theology,* I, p. 21.

15. *Jesus and the Word,* p. 29.

16. *Ibid.,* p. 170; *Theology,* I, pp. 28 f.

17. *Theology,* I, p. 31.

18. *Ibid.,* p. 27; *Jesus and the Word,* pp. 19–25; *Primitive Christianity,* p. 90.

19. *Primitive Christianity,* p. 90; *Theology,* I, p. 9.

20. *Theology,* I, pp. 29 f. Schweitzer proposed to explain the absence of Jesus' predictions of his return as Son of Man by the theory that Jesus felt no need to reveal this "secret" of his future office to his hearers; when the Kingdom comes, which will be soon, they will learn it. Schweitzer concluded that Jesus expected that his removal from the earth would be accomplished through a violent death!

21. The question of Jesus' "messianic self-consciousness" con-

tinues to be debated, sometimes in terms of his "understanding of existence." No final answer seems in sight. Bultmann concedes that "the question as to whether Jesus knew himself as Messiah remains open," but maintains his *opinion* that Jesus did not believe himself to be the Messiah or the Messiah-to-come ("Is Exegesis Without Presuppositions Possible?" [1957], in *Existence and Faith,* p. 290).

22. "Indeed, Jesus demands decision with reference to his ministry. . . . If Paul, like the earliest community, saw in Jesus the Messiah, *he did nothing other than affirm Jesus' own claim* that man's destiny is decided with reference to his person." ("Jesus and Paul," p. 196, italics added.)

23. *Theology,* I, p. 43.

24. Bultmann himself summarizes "with a bit of caution" what may be known of Jesus' activity in "Primitive Christian Kerygma," pp. 22 ff. Schubert Ogden has pointed to several sections of *Jesus and the Word* that further characterize Jesus' ministry, in "Bultmann and the 'New Quest,'" *The Journal of Bible and Religion,* Vol. XXX (1962), p. 217n10. See also Van Harvey and Schubert Ogden, "How New Is the 'New Quest of the Historical Jesus'?" in Braaten and Harrisville, *op. cit.,* p. 205n21. Ogden cogently criticizes Bultmann's claim that the new quest is "impossible" in "Bultmann and the 'New Quest,'" pp. 214 ff. See also Hans Conzelmann in "The Method of the Life-of-Jesus Research," in Braaten and Harrisville, *op. cit.,* pp. 56 f.

25. *Jesus and the Word,* p. 38.

26. *Ibid.,* p. 51; *Theology,* I, p. 7; *Primitive Christianity,* p. 90; "Primitive Christian Kerygma," pp. 16, 23, 28.

27. *Theology,* I, p. 22.

28. *Primitive Christianity,* p. 86.

29. The category "Either-Or" comes to Bultmann from Kierkegaard.

30. *Primitive Christianity,* p. 90.

31. *Jesus and the Word,* p. 32.

32. *Ibid.,* pp. 83 f., 78.

33. *Ibid.,* p. 92; *Theology,* I, p. 12. Also, *Jesus and the Word,* p. 77.

34. E.g., Thomas C. Oden, *Radical Obedience: The Ethics of Rudolf Bultmann* (The Westminster Press, 1964).

35. "Reply," in Charles W. Kegley (ed.), *The Theology of Rudolf Bultmann* (Harper & Row, Publishers, Inc., 1966), p. 283.

36. *Jesus and the Word,* p. 113; also p. 118.

37. *Theology,* I, p. 18, also p. 21; and "Jesus and Paul," p. 191.

38. *Jesus and the Word,* pp. 114 f.

39. *Ibid.,* p. 115.

40. *Ibid.,* pp. 117 f.

41. *Ibid.,* p. 117.

42. *Ibid.,* p. 113, italics added. See also pp. 93 f., and "Reply," p. 279.

43. *Jesus and the Word,* p. 109, also p. 112: "The basis of Jesus' demand for love is . . . the concept of obedience, of renunciation of one's own claim." "Jesus thought of love . . . as an overcoming of self-will in the concrete situation of life in which a man encounters other men."

44. *Ibid.,* p. 112. See also *This World and the Beyond: Marburg Sermons,* tr. by H. Knight (Charles Scribner's Sons, 1960), p. 132: Men "must flee again and again to [God's] grace in order to have any value."

45. *Jesus and the Word,* pp. 117 f., italics added. See also p. 114: "As obedient to God, setting aside my selfish will, renouncing my own claims, I stand before my neighbor, prepared for sacrifice *for my neighbor* as for God" (italics added). Also *Primitive Christianity,* p. 92: In responding to "the commandment of love . . . a man turns away from self and places himself at the disposal of others."

46. Harnack, *What Is Christianity?* p. 72.

47. *Jesus and the Word,* p. 85, italics added.

48. *Ibid.,* p. 88.

49. *Ibid.*

50. *Ibid.*

51. *Ibid.*

52. *Theology,* I, p. 24; also *Primitive Christianity,* p. 78; and *Jesus and the Word,* pp. 93, 101 f.

53. *Jesus and the Word,* pp. 88, 93, 108, 113.

54. *Ibid.,* p. 97, italics added.

55. *Ibid.,* p. 98.

56. *Ibid.,* p. 107.

57. Cf. Heinz-Horst Schrey's critique, "The Consequences of Bultmann's Theology for Ethics," in Kegley, *op. cit.,* esp. p. 196.

58. *Jesus and the Word,* p. 109.

59. *Primitive Christianity,* p. 75.

60. *Ibid.:* "The parable of the Good Samaritan shows that there is no difficulty in seeing what *we* ought to do when *our* neighbor needs

our help. The phrase 'as thyself' indicates both the unlimited measure and the direction of love as a *principle of conduct. We* all know how *we* would like others to treat *us* if *we* were in the same situation *ourselves*" (italics added). Here it is evident that Bultmann regards Jesus' words as significant not only for his hearers but also for *us.* See also *Jesus and the Word,* p. 115.

61. *Jesus Christ and Mythology* (Charles Scribner's Sons, 1958), p. 18; hereafter cited as *Mythology.* Evidently he means that these demands should be relevant to the moral life of modern men.

62. "Jesus and Paul," p. 187.

63. "Today nobody doubts that Jesus' conception of the Kingdom of God is an eschatological one—at least in European theology and, as far as I can see, also among American New Testament scholars." (*Mythology,* p. 13.)

64. *Jesus and the Word,* p. 126.

65. *Ibid.,* p. 129.

66. *Ibid.,* pp. 127, 129; *Theology,* I, p. 20.

67. Schweitzer, *Mystery,* pp. 53 ff.

68. Bultmann has recently acknowledged his continuing positive orientation toward "liberal theology": "Autobiographical Reflections" in Kegley, *op. cit.,* p. xxiv.

69. "Jesus and Paul," p. 186.

70. Bultmann's use of the term "myth" is notoriously ambiguous. See Robert H. Ayers, " 'Myth' in Theological Discourse: A Profusion of Confusion," in *Anglican Theological Review,* Vol. XLVIII (1966), pp. 200–217.

71. *Primitive Christianity,* p. 92, italics added. Also *Jesus and the Word,* pp. 55 f.; and *Mythology,* pp. 25 f. Obviously, Bultmann means that Jesus' understanding of life "stands" despite the failure of his eschatological misconception.

72. "Jesus and Paul," p. 186; *Theology,* I, pp. 22 ff.

73. *Jesus and the Word,* p. 131, italics added.

74. *Ibid.,* pp. 55 f.

75. *Ibid.,* pp. 52, 55; *Primitive Christianity,* p. 92.

76. *Theology,* I, pp. 25 f.

77. *Jesus and the Word,* p. 52. Also, p. 55: "The eschatological message of Jesus . . . can be understood only when one considers the *conception of man which in the last analysis underlies it*" (Bultmann's italics). See also p. 131; "Jesus and Paul," p. 186; *Primitive Christianity,* p. 92; and *Mythology,* p. 26.

78. *Jesus and the Word,* p. 131. Also *Primitive Christianity,* p. 75: "His demand is always present anew in each successive encounter with our neighbour."

79. A few times, Bultmann implies that Jesus' idea of eschatology is unique or distinctive, in contrast to that of his contemporaries, in the certainty or assurance with which he proclaimed that *now* the time has come, that God's reign is "breaking in" (*Primitive Christianity,* pp. 87 f.; *Theology,* I, p. 6). But such certainty could not have been unique, for as Bultmann himself points out, the Baptist, who had been at work before Jesus came on the scene, and gave Jesus his "first impetus," was a preacher of repentance, crying out, "Repent ye, for the Reign of God has drawn nigh" (*Primitive Christianity,* p. 76).

80. *Mythology,* p. 26; *Jesus and the Word,* p. 52.

81. *Jesus and the Word,* pp. 55 f.

82. *Ibid.,* p. 52.

83. Matt. 24:36 to 25:13; Luke 12:35–48.

84. E.g., Matt. 6:19; 7:24 ff.; 19:21; 25:14–46.

85. "A Reply to J. Schniewind," in H. W. Bartsch (ed.), *Kerygma and Myth,* tr. by R. H. Fuller (Harper & Row, Publishers, Inc., 1961), p. 106.

86. *Primitive Christianity,* p. 75. One wonders what Old Testament text, if any, Bultmann had in mind. As a Lutheran, he overestimates the importance of "reward" in the Old Testament, and underestimates it in the New Testament. See also *Jesus and the Word,* p. 129; and *Theology,* I, p. 20. In the latter and also in *Primitive Christianity,* he repeats or paraphrases much of what he had previously written in *Jesus and the Word.* His interpretation of the historical Jesus shows little change during the twenty-five years between the first and the last of these books. So Ogden has also argued recently against James M. Robinson in "Bultmann and the 'New Quest,'" p. 211.

87. *Jesus and the Word,* p. 129. Bultmann chooses to ignore the evident meaning of Matt. 23:13–15, 33; 5:46; Luke 6:32–35!

88. *Theology,* I, p. 9.

89. *Primitive Christianity,* p. 91.

90. *Theology,* I, p. 20, italics added.

91. *Ibid.* Neither Weiss nor Schweitzer, of course, so characterized the "conditions of admittance." In Schweitzer's view, it was "the

moral disposition which justifies admission into the Kingdom" (*Mystery,* p. 54).

92. *Theology,* I, pp. 20 f.; *Jesus and the Word,* p. 122. Note that Schweitzer spoke of a morally transformed disposition. This is not far removed from Bultmann's notion of "radical obedience."

93. *Primitive Christianity,* p. 79; *Theology,* I, p. 25.

94. *Jesus and the Word,* p. 54. See also p. 120: "Man's decision has a final character; he becomes thereby a righteous man or a sinner." See also pp. 51 and 132; and *Primitive Christianity,* p. 93.

95. *Jesus and the Word,* p. 79; *Theology,* I, pp. 14 f.

96. *Jesus and the Word,* p. 80; but cf. p. 54: "Only what a man now does gives him his value."

97. *Ibid.,* p. 121.

98. *Theology,* I, p. 14.

99. *Ibid.,* p. 15, italics added.

100. Occasionally Bultmann does not make it clear that Jesus understood that only those who survived the judgment would participate in the Kingdom, as if the possibility of an adverse judgment and exclusion from the Kingdom had no real place in Jesus' preaching or "understanding of existence," e.g., *Jesus and the Word,* pp. 35, 215, 217; *Theology,* I, pp. 24, 27; *Mythology,* p. 27.

101. "Primitive Christian Kerygma," p. 30, also, pp. 41 f.

102. *Theology,* I, p. 3; *Primitive Christianity,* p. 93.

103. The Braaten and Harrisville volume, *The Historical Jesus and the Kerygmatic Christ,* is particularly recommended, especially the first chapter by Bultmann and the last by Harvey and Ogden; also P. Joseph Cahill, S.J., "Rudolf Bultmann and Post-Bultmann Tendencies," in M. E. Marty and D. G. Peerman (eds.), *New Theology,* Vol. II (The Macmillan Company, 1965), pp. 222–254.

104. *Primitive Christianity,* p. 93; "Reply," p. 260.

105. "Reply," pp. 260 f., also pp. 272 f.

106. "Primitive Christian Kerygma," p. 30, quoted above, p. 100.

107. *Ibid.,* p. 41.

108. *Ibid.,* p. 42.

109. *Ibid.,* p. 38. Bultmann's argument at this point is visibly fallacious. He asks, in effect, why, "if the proclamation of Jesus places the hearer before a decision and offers him the possibility of a new existence," the apostles did not simply repeat his teaching/proclamation instead of preaching about him. For one thing, the apostles did repeat Jesus' words, notably in the Synoptic Gospels,

which Bultmann occasionally will admit are part of the church's kerygma! His confusion on this point is well illustrated by the following sentence: "Indeed [the Synoptic Gospels] do not intend to be read as historical reports, but as a portion of proclamation, which is true also of Luke, though he intends to give a historical report" (p. 21). In the second place, the church obviously could not be content simply to continue repeating Jesus' words. The whole situation had changed: Jesus' death and their experiences of his resurrection needed to be accounted for. Who was he? What had become of him? Would they see him again, and would the Kingdom come after all? Questions of this sort demanded answers, and answers were offered in the early Christian preaching and writing, but there is no evidence that such answers were intended to replace the message of Jesus.

110. E.g., *ibid.*, p. 25: "Faith does not at all arise from the acceptance of historical facts. That would only lead to legitimizing, whereas the kerygma really calls for faith."

111. Cahill, *loc. cit.*, p. 237.

112. Harvey and Ogden, *loc. cit.*, pp. 229 f.

113. *Ibid.*, p. 232.

114. "Primitive Christian Kerygma," p. 16.

115. *Ibid.*, p. 18. The latter understanding he attributes to Paul and John. Here, as in most of Bultmann's summaries of the kerygma, there is no reference to the future as the time when Christ will come or the end of the age will take place. There is no room in Bultmann's existentialist philosophy for actual future events, and so there is no place for such events in the early church's kerygma—at least not in Bultmann's version of it!

116. *Marburg Sermons*, pp. 63, 109, 161; "Reply," p. 271.

117. "Reply," p. 258; "Primitive Christian Kerygma," pp. 25, 30.

118. James M. Robinson, "The Recent Debate on the 'New Quest,'" *The Journal of Bible and Religion*, Vol. XXX (1962), pp. 206 f.

119. "Primitive Christian Kerygma," p. 42.

120. *Ibid.*, pp. 19 ff.

121. *Marburg Sermons*, pp. 24 ff., 28.

122. *Ibid.*, p. 33.

123. *Ibid.*, p. 122.

124. *Ibid.*, p. 145.

125. *Ibid.*, p. 147.

126. Other examples in the *Marburg Sermons* are on pp. 133, 149, 171, 176 f., 181 f.

127. Carl Michalson, *Worldly Theology* (Charles Scribner's Sons, 1967), p. 83.

128. *Primitive Christianity,* p. 75, also p. 77.

129. *Mythology,* pp. 17 f., 31.

130. "Reply to J. Schniewind," p. 117. See also the first sentence in *Theology,* I, p. 3.

131. *Jesus and the Word,* p. 8. See also p. 11: "[Jesus' words] meet *us* with the question of how we are to interpret our own existence."

132. *Ibid.,* p. 123, italics added.

133. *Ibid.,* p. 77.

134. *Ibid.,* p. 115. Note Bultmann's use of the first person singular. It is evident on this and nearby pages where Bultmann uses the first and second persons, and speaks generally of "man" in the present tense, that he has in view the meaning of Jesus' "double command of love" for the moral life of *modern* men.

135. "Das christliche Gebot der Nächstenliebe" (1930), in *Glauben und Verstehen* (Tübingen: J. C. B. Mohr, 1933), Vol. I, pp. 229–244.

136. *Ibid.,* pp. 229 f. Cf. *Jesus and the Word,* pp. 73, 84: Jesus' ethic "is an ethic of obedience."

137. "Das christliche Gebot," *passim.* Cf. *Jesus and the Word,* pp. 114 f.; and "Humanism and Christianity" in *Essays: Philosophical and Theological,* tr. by J. C. G. Greig (London: SCM Press, Ltd., 1955), p. 155: "It [God's demanding will] is always met with afresh in a new form in the encounters of human intercourse in which at any given time my decision is demanded—my decision to live for the person I am meeting as my 'neighbor' at that particular time. This living for one's neighbor is called *love;* and it is a love . . . based . . . in responsiveness to that in which my 'neighbor' has need of me, at a given time."

138. "Das christliche Gebot," p. 238; *Jesus and the Word,* p. 112. See also *Presence of Eternity: History and Eschatology* (Harper & Brothers, 1957), p. 152: "All responsible decisions are born of love. For love consists in unreservedly being for one's neighbour and this is possible only for the man who has become free from himself."

139. "Das christliche Gebot," p. 238.

140. *Jesus and the Word,* p. 115.

141. "Das christliche Gebot," p. 239.

142. *Jesus and the Word,* pp. 84, 94; see also p. 113.

143. *Theology,* I, pp. 330 ff.; II, pp. 78 ff.

144. "Response," in Oden, *op. cit.,* p. 147.

145. Bultmann emphatically (and properly) insists that Jesus was no teacher of timeless values, ideals, or virtues; e.g., *Jesus and the Word,* pp. 84, 88, 105, 108, 112.

146. E.g., *ibid.,* pp. 112 f., 118.

147. *History and Eschatology,* p. 152; "Humanism and Christianity," in *Essays,* p. 155.

148. *Theology,* I, p. 15; *History and Eschatology,* p. 44; "Humanism and Christianity," p. 158.

149. *Jesus and the Word,* p. 88.

150. "Response," p. 145.

151. Schrey, *op. cit.,* pp. 196 ff.

152. "Autobiographical Reflections," in Kegley, *op. cit.,* p. xxii.

153. *Marburg Sermons,* pp. 113, 120, 166, 177.

154. *Ibid.,* p. 216, also p. 230; "Autobiographical Reflections," pp. xxi f.

155. *Marburg Sermons,* pp. 148 f.; *Primitive Christianity,* p. 75.

156. "Reply," p. 280.

157. "The Sermon on the Mount and the Justice of the State" (1936), in *Existence and Faith,* p. 204.

Chapter IV. Recent British and American Interpretations

1. "The Framework of the Gospel Narrative" (1932), in *New Testament Studies* (Manchester: Manchester University Press, 1953), pp. 4 ff.; hereafter cited as "Framework."

2. *Ibid.,* p. 11. See also *The Gospels as History: A Reconsideration,* reprinted from the *Bulletin of the John Rylands Library,* Vol. XXII (Manchester: Manchester University Press, 1938), p. 15; hereafter cited as *Reconsideration.*

3. "Framework," pp. 6–10. Dodd also considers it possible to find in or behind the Fourth Gospel "an ancient tradition" of historical merit concerning the life of Jesus: *Historical Tradition in the Fourth Gospel* (London: Cambridge University Press, 1963), p. 423.

4. *Reconsideration,* pp. 18, 24; see also *The Parables of the Kingdom* (London: James Nisbet & Co., Ltd., 1938; rev. ed., Charles Scribner's Sons, 1961), p. 40; hereafter cited as *The Parables.* Dodd did not change his basic position in his revised edition of *The*

Parables of the Kingdom which was published in 1961. All quotations here are from the 1938 edition, reprinted in 1950, and are used by permission of the publishers, James Nisbet & Co., Ltd., and Charles Scribner's Sons.

5. *The Parables,* p. 104.

6. "Framework," p. 5. The theory that Jesus' Galilean ministry was unsuccessful is, according to Schweitzer, one of the enduring fictions created by the writers of the nineteenth-century "liberal lives of Jesus." See Schweitzer, *Out of My Life and Thought,* pp. 35 ff.

7. *About the Gospels* (London: Cambridge University Press, 1950), pp. 3 f., italics added. What the italicized words are intended to mean is not clear. Is Dodd suggesting that a political messianic movement was growing in support of Jesus, or that his life was in danger?

8. *History and the Gospel* (London: James Nisbet & Co., Ltd., 1938), p. 132; hereafter cited as *History.*

9. *About the Gospels,* p. 7.

10. *The Parables,* p. 42.

11. *The Parables,* p. 107; see also "The Kingdom of God and History," in H. G. Wood, C. H. Dodd, *et al., The Kingdom of God and History* (Willett, Clark & Company, 1938), p. 34.

12. *The Apostolic Preaching* (Willett, Clark & Company, 1937), p. 161.

13. *The Parables,* pp. 189, 200–202.

14. *Ibid.,* p. 44. The Marcan parallel, Mark 3:26, hypothesizes that Satan's kingdom "is coming to an end" or "has an end" (*telos echei*). In all Synoptic versions it is clear that Satan's house, though doomed, is not yet ended. In that case, is the Kingdom of God yet realized *on earth?* Matthew did not so understand it: Matt. 12:32 distinguishes between "the present age" and "the coming age."

15. The relation between *engizein* and *naga'* or *meta',* however, is not so decisive as Dodd would like to believe. In the LXX *engizein* much more frequently translates *nagash* or *qarabh,* which mean "to approach" or "draw near." See Edwin Hatch and Henry A. Redpath, *A Concordance to the Septuagint* (Graz: Akademische Druck- u. Verlagsanstalt, 1954), Vol. I, pp. 362 f. See also the critique of Dodd by W. G. Kümmel, *Promise and Fulfilment* (London: SCM Press, Ltd., 1957), pp. 19–25.

16. *The Parables,* p. 48.

17. *Ibid.*

18. *Ibid.*, pp. v f.

19. Before he thought of the theory of "realized eschatology" Dodd translated Luke 17:20 f.: "The Kingdom of God is within you" (*The Gospel in the New Testament* [London: National Sunday School Union, 1926], p. 37). He understood it to mean what both Harnack and the "social gospel" liberals had supposed: "The Kingdom of God in the hearts of men—even in the hearts of a very few—is the germ from which the better order of the Good Time Coming must grow. . . . There is a direct and organic connection between the presence of God's rule in a sincere and childlike heart and the final triumph of His cause in all the world" (pp. 38 f.).

20. *The Parables,* p. 49, italics added.

21. *Gospel in the N.T.*, p. 34; see also *The Parables,* pp. 49, 102, 185; "Kingdom of God and History," p. 34.

22. *The Parables,* pp. 103 f.

23. *Ibid.*, pp. vi, 48, quoted above.

24. *Ibid.*, p. 49.

25. *Ibid.*, p. 138.

26. *Ibid.*, pp. 53 f.

27. But see below, pp. 123 f.

28. *The Parables,* pp. 104 f.

29. *Ibid.*, p. 105.

30. *Gospel in the N.T.*, p. 19.

31. *Ibid.;* see also pp. 22 f., 26, 32, 38 f.

32. *The Parables,* p. 47.

33. *Ibid.*, p. 108, also pp. 121, 197.

34. *Ibid.*, p. 42, but see pp. 34 f.

35. *Ibid.*, p. vii: "They [the Gospels] interpret life to us, by initiating us into a situation in which, as Christians believe, the eternal was uniquely manifested in time, a situation therefore which is both history at its decisive moment (decisive for us, too), and eternal fact, universal and contemporary in the deepest possible sense. It is this situation that the parables . . . were *designed* to illustrate." Italics added.

36. *Ibid.*, pp. 109, 197 f., italics added.

37. *Ibid.*, pp. 30 ff., 136 ff. Also p. 201: Each man "must make up his mind there and then to do something about it, before all opportunity for action is at an end."

38. *Ibid.*, pp. 51 f., 66, 70, 170 ff.

39. *Ibid.*, p. 153.

40. *Apostolic Preaching,* pp. 58 f.

41. *The Parables,* p. 56.

42. *Ibid.,* p. 58. He mentions the verse in *Historical Tradition in the Fourth Gospel* (p. 378), but disclaims any notion as to the "original intention" of the saying.

43. *The Parables,* p. 45. See also "The Ethics of the New Testament," in Ruth N. Anshen (ed.), *Moral Principles of Action* (Harper & Brothers, 1952), p. 553; hereafter cited as "Ethics." He maintains elsewhere that Luke 10:12 is a prediction of "the horrors of war and social upheaval," but admits that the judgment of Sodom and Gommorah presents a problem for this interpretation: *The Parables,* pp. 81 f.

44. *The Parables,* p. 49. Cf. Harnack, *What Is Christianity?* pp. 53 f.

45. *The Parables,* p. 83.

46. *Gospel in the N.T.,* p. 29. See also *The Gospel and the Law of Christ* (London: Longmans, Green & Co., Ltd., 1947), p. 20; hereafter cited as *Law of Christ.* Also *Gospel and Law* (Columbia University Press, 1951), p. 81.

47. *The Parables,* pp. 76 f., 189, 200–202.

48. *Law of Christ,* p. 18; *Gospel and Law,* p. 74. Martin Dibelius had supposed that Jesus' teaching was the ethic of the *future* Kingdom of God in his *The Sermon on the Mount* (Charles Scribner's Sons, 1940).

49. *History,* p. 125; "Ethics," p. 554. Also *The Parables,* p. 109; and *Gospel and Law,* pp. 60–62.

50. *Law of Christ,* p. 13; also "Ethics," p. 557.

51. *Gospel and Law,* pp. 55, 60 f.; "Ethics," p. 553; *History,* p. 126; see also *Law of Christ,* pp. 16 f.

52. *Gospel and Law,* p. 61, also p. 76.

53. *Law of Christ,* pp. 16 f. and *passim.* Dodd considers much of the tradition in the Fourth Gospel authentic: see *Law of Christ,* pp. 11 f.

54. *Gospel and Law,* pp. 39 ff.

55. *Law of Christ,* p. 16.

56. *Gospel and Law,* p. 83.

57. *Gospel and Law,* p. 73. Dodd regularly places the accent over the final syllable. See also "Ethics," p. 555: "The fundamental obligation resting upon subjects of God's reign is to reproduce, in the varied situations of human life in society, the quality and direction characteristic of the character and action of God as He meets us in

the coming of His Kingdom, and thereby to fulfill the true role allotted to men in God's design, that of 'sons of the Father in Heaven.'" The "coming of His Kingdom" here seems to mean the coming of Jesus Christ.

58. *Gospel and Law,* pp. 59–62.

59. *Ibid.,* p. 62; also "Ethics," p. 558.

60. *History,* p. 127.

61. *Gospel and Law,* p. 62. Also, p. 64: "They are intended to offer positive moral guidance for action, to those who have, in the words of the gospels, received the Kingdom of God."

62. *About the Gospels,* pp. 28 f. See also *History,* pp. 127 f.: "They stand for the unattainable which we are bound to strive to attain. . . . The ethical precepts of Jesus are . . . a guide to the good life, in the sense that they set before us the goal which determines the true direction of moral effort."

63. *Law of Christ,* p. 19; *Gospel and Law,* pp. 77, 81 f.

64. *Law of Christ,* pp. 17 f.; *Gospel and Law,* p. 73.

65. "Ethics," p. 558.

66. *Thirty Years of New Testament Study* (1950), reprint from the May issue of *Union Seminary Quarterly Review,* Vol. V (1950), p. 8: "The yawning gap which earlier criticism left between the Jesus of History and the emergent Church disappears."

67. Harvey Cox, *The Secular City* (The Macmillan Company, 1965), pp. 112, 125, 191.

68. James H. Smylie, "Sons of God in the City," in Daniel Callahan (ed.), *The Secular City Debate* (The Macmillan Company, 1966), p. 11; Harvey Cox, "Cox on His Critics," in Callahan, *op. cit.,* p. 87. Cox maintains his optimism by selectivity: e.g., he chooses New Delhi not Calcutta (where hundreds lie dying in the streets) when he discusses the blessings of secular city in India. Writing on the 1967 summer ghetto riots in *Christianity and Crisis,* Cox seems less hopeful about the human prospect.

69. Thomas J. J. Altizer and William Hamilton, *Radical Theology and the Death of God* (The Bobbs-Merrill Company, Inc., 1966), pp. 183 ff.

70. Thomas J. J. Altizer, *The Gospel of Christian Atheism* (The Westminster Press, 1966), pp. 136, 156; Altizer and Hamilton, *Radical Theology,* p. 188.

71. Altizer and Hamilton, *Radical Theology,* pp. 157 f., 165, 169.

72. William Temple, *Christian Faith and Life* (London: SCM

Press, Ltd., 1957), p. 138. As early as 1913, Temple expressed characteristic Anglo-Saxon anxiety about the futuristic eschatological interpretation of the Kingdom: "If I thought He [Jesus] expected an immediate catastrophe other than His own death and Resurrection, I think I should have to renounce Christianity." Cited in Joseph Fletcher, *William Temple* (The Seabury Press, Inc., 1963), p. 38.

73. One might also mention Walter E. Bundy, Millar Burrows, B. S. Easton, R. H. Fuller, and Krister Stendahl. Several European writers, aside from Schweitzer's "school," also concur: e.g., M. Goguel, M. Dibelius, H. Windisch.

74. E.g., John Knox, *Jesus: Lord and Christ* (Harper & Brothers, 1958), pp. 88, 104; Paul Ramsey, *Basic Christian Ethics* (Charles Scribner's Sons, 1950), pp. 25 ff.; William Manson, *The Way of the Cross* (John Knox Press, 1964), pp. 40–44.

75. John Baillie, *The Place of Jesus Christ in Modern Christianity* (Charles Scribner's Sons, 1930), p. 172.

76. Joseph Fletcher, *Situation Ethics* (The Westminster Press, 1966), p. 139: "Modern Christians ought not to be naïve enough to accept any other view of Jesus' ethic than the situational one." Schweitzer found it a mark of the liberal writers to ignore eschatology and claim Jesus' sanction for their own respective theories.

77. *Ibid.*, pp. 83, 162. The source is Schweitzer's *Philosophy of Civilization*, p. 318.

78. For example, T. W. Manson, in H. D. A. Major, T. W. Manson, and C. J. Wright, *The Mission and Message of Jesus* (E. P. Dutton & Company, Inc., 1938), p. 329; Amos N. Wilder, *Eschatology and Ethics in the Teaching of Jesus* (Harper & Brothers, 1950), p. 178; John Knox, *Jesus: Lord and Christ*, p. 109, and *The Ethics of Jesus in the Teaching of the Church* (Abingdon Press, 1961), pp. 39, 45 f.; Georgia Harkness, *Christian Ethics* (Abingdon Press, 1957), p. 63; Albert Knudson, *The Principles of Christian Ethics* (Abingdon-Cokesbury Press, 1943), p. 42; E. F. Scott, *The Ethical Teaching of Jesus* (The Macmillan Company, 1936), p. 43; E. Clinton Gardner, *Biblical Faith and Social Ethics* (Harper & Row, Publishers, Inc., 1960), pp. 62 f.; A. M. Hunter, *Introducing New Testament Theology* (The Westminster Press, 1958), p. 37, and *The Work and Words of Jesus* (The Westminster Press, 1951), pp. 12 f.; Reinhold Niebuhr, *An Interpretation of Christian Ethics* (Meridian Books, Inc., 1956), p. 58; John Bright, *The Kingdom of God* (Abingdon-Cokesbury

Press, 1953), pp. 222 f.; Norman Perrin, *The Kingdom of God in the Teaching of Jesus* (The Westminster Press, 1963), pp. 43 f.; G. E. Ladd, *Jesus and the Kingdom* (Harper & Row, Publishers, Inc., 1964), pp. 121 f.; C. J. Cadoux, *The Historic Mission of Jesus* (Harper & Brothers, n.d.), p. 126; G. F. Thomas, *Christian Ethics and Moral Philosophy* (Charles Scribner's Sons, 1955), p. 30; Paul Ramsey, *Basic Christian Ethics,* p. 30.

79. These and certain other misunderstandings of Schweitzer's interim ethics theory are reviewed in my article "Interim Ethics," pp. 220–233.

80. Scott, *op. cit.,* p. 45.

81. Cadoux, *op. cit.,* p. 115; Major, Manson, and Wright, *op. cit.,* p. 328.

82. Hunter, *Introducing,* p. 39; Harkness, *op. cit.,* p. 56. Italics added.

83. J. A. T. Robinson, *Honest to God* (The Westminster Press, 1963), p. 112, italics added.

84. Knox, *Ethics,* p. 46.

85. *Ibid.,* pp. 18, 20, 23, 34, 42, 50, 105.

86. Morton S. Enslin, *The Prophet from Nazareth* (McGraw-Hill Book Company, Inc., 1961), p. 8.

87. T. W. Manson, *The Teaching of Jesus* (London: Cambridge University Press, 1935), p. 135.

88. Perrin, *op. cit.,* p. 203, also, p. 187.

89. Manson, *Teaching,* pp. 130 f.

90. T. W. Manson, "Realized Eschatology and the Messianic Secret," in D. E. Nineham (ed.), *Studies in the Gospels* (Oxford: Basil Blackwell & Mott, Ltd., 1955), pp. 210, 221 f., and *The Servant-Messiah* (London: Cambridge University Press, 1953), p. 88.

91. A. M. Hunter, *Introducing,* pp. 39 ff. So also William Barclay, *The Mind of Christ* (London: SCM Press, Ltd., 1960), p. 61.

92. Wilder, *op. cit.,* pp. 89, 113, 141.

93. *Ibid.,* pp. 92, 116, 128 f., 161. Cf. Schleiermacher. See also Gardner, *op. cit.,* p. 65.

94. Cox, *Secular City,* pp. 111 ff. George W. Peck properly chastises Cox for *"Doctor ex machina"* methodology in his review, "The Secular City and the Bible," in Callahan, *op. cit.,* pp. 43 f. Another example is Cox's citation of unidentified "German scholars" on behalf of the plausible theory of *"sich realisierende Eschatologie,"* from

which he leaps to the implausible conclusion that "then we live today in a world where . . . the coming of the Kingdom *still* occurs" (*Secular City,* p. 113).

95. Cadoux, *op. cit.,* p. 128; Barclay, *op. cit.,* p. 63; Altizer and Hamilton, *op. cit.,* p. 188; Knox, *Jesus: Lord,* pp. 17, 104.

96. Cadoux, *op. cit.,* pp. 128 f.; Barclay, *op. cit.,* p. 63.

97. Manson, *Teaching,* pp. 286, 299, 301; Major, Manson, and Wright, *op. cit.,* pp. 328 f.

98. Wilder, *op. cit.,* p. 160.

99. Major, Manson, and Wright, *op. cit.,* p. 328.

100. Hunter, *Work and Words,* p. 77: "The ethic of the Sermon on the Mount is *the moral idea* of the Kingdom of God." Perrin, *op. cit.,* p. 206: "Jesus . . . ventures to declare the paradise-will of God now valid."

101. Enslin, *op cit.,* p. 14, also, p. 217.

102. Manson, *The Way of the Cross,* p. 60.

103. Knox, *Jesus: Lord,* p. 109; also Ramsey, *Basic Christian Ethics,* p. 39.

104. Ramsey, *Basic Christian Ethics,* pp. 39–42.

105. Knox, *Jesus: Lord,* p. 111.

106. Ramsey, *Basic Christian Ethics,* p. 42.

107. Some, however, speak of the demands of the (realized) Kingdom of God. For instance, Hunter, *Introducing,* p. 38; Robinson, *Honest,* p. 111; Cox, *Secular City,* p. 113; Ramsey, *Basic Christian Ethics,* p. 30. Against these, it should be pointed out that in the New Testament, *Jesus* demands, and speaks of what *God* demands, but nowhere does *the Kingdom* demand anything.

108. Robinson, *Honest,* p. 76.

109. *Ibid.,* p. 82, also p. 114. Cf. Ramsey, *op. cit.,* pp. 19 f.

110. Paul M. van Buren, *The Secular Meaning of the Gospel* (The Macmillan Company, 1963), p. 138, also pp. 123, 132, 163.

111. H. Richard Niebuhr, *Radical Monotheism and Western Culture* (Harper & Row, Publishers, Inc., 1960).

112. Van Buren, *op. cit.,* p. 143.

113. Niebuhr, *Radical Monotheism,* esp. Chs. 1 and 2; van Buren, *op. cit.,* p. 142.

114. William Hamilton, *The New Essence of Christianity* (Association Press, 1961), pp. 109, 112.

115. Altizer and Hamilton, *op. cit.,* pp. 37, 49 f.

116. *Ibid.,* pp. 178, 182 ff.

117. H. Richard Niebuhr, *The Responsible Self* (Harper & Row, Publishers, Inc., 1963), pp. 154 ff.

118. H. Richard Niebuhr, *Christ and Culture* (Harper & Brothers, 1951), p. 21.

119. Niebuhr, *Responsible Self,* pp. 166 f., also *Radical Monotheism,* p. 42.

120. Temple, *op. cit.,* p. 47.

121. As previously noted, C. H. Dodd; Paul Ramsey, *Deeds and Rules in Christian Ethics* (Charles Scribner's Sons, 1967), pp. 32 f.

122. Fletcher, *Situation Ethics,* p. 68, also pp. 86, 129. He imputes (mistakenly) this idea to William Temple (*William Temple,* p. 160). Ramsey notes Fletcher's desire to convert Bonhoeffer, Brunner, and Barth into "situationists" (*Deeds and Rules,* pp. 154 ff.).

123. Robinson, *Honest,* pp. 112–118.

124. *Ibid.,* pp. 115, 118, italics added; also p. 119.

125. Ramsey, *Basic Christian Ethics,* pp. 56 ff., 99 f.

126. Hunter, *Introducing,* p. 39.

127. Knox, *Ethics,* pp. 44 f., 106. Cf. Bultmann's "radical obedience."

128. "The Center of Value," in Ruth Anshen, *op. cit.,* reprinted in Niebuhr, *Radical Monotheism,* as supplementary essay No. II.

Chapter V. Jesus, Ethics, and the Present Situation

1. Cynthia L. Smith, "Synoptic Eschatology." Unpublished paper, University of Florida, 1966.

2. Dodd, *Gospel and Law,* pp. 55, 61, 76.

3. Dodd, *Apostolic Preaching,* pp. 162 f.

4. E.g., Oden, *op. cit.,* pp. 14–24. But see, e.g., Reinhold Niebuhr, *The Irony of American History* (Charles Scribner's Sons, 1952), pp. 157 ff.

5. The term was coined and emphasized by Prof. Ralph Turner of Yale.

6. See above, p. 95.

7. Ramsey and Fletcher to the contrary. See below, pp. 161 f.

8. Matt. 5:43–48; cf. John 13:34 f. Christians have found it difficult enough to love one another, let alone their enemies: I John 2:1–11; 3:10–24.

9. Cf. Schweitzer, *Philosophy of Civilization,* pp. 299, 305.

10. Martin Buber, *Between Man and Man* (Beacon Press, Inc., 1955), pp. 167 ff.

11. Cox, *Secular City*, p. 202.

12. Above, pp. 87 f., 111 f.

13. Fletcher, *Situation Ethics*, pp. 125, 135 f.

14. *Ibid.*, pp. 71, 126, 132.

15. Cf. Ramsey, *Basic Christian Ethics*, p. 59: "Jesus' actions and teaching may be described as flowing from an orientation which valued the needs of the neighbor above all else." Love does not cease in the Messianic age when there will be no more unfulfilled needs! (Cf. I Cor. 13:8 ff.)

16. Ramsey, *Deeds*, p. 159; Robinson, *Honest*, p. 119.

17. Ramsey, *Basic Christian Ethics*, pp. 40, 42.

18. Fletcher, *Situation Ethics*, pp. 75, 124 f., 135 f.

19. Fletcher explicitly denies that guilt is involved (*ibid.*, p. 124).

20. Schweitzer, *Philosophy of Civilization*, esp. pp. 316–327.

21. *Ibid.*, p. 318. Fletcher acknowledges that he had not read these words in their original context (*Situation Ethics*, p. 83).

22. Jer. 31:33 f. See also Hos. 2:18–20; Isa. 11:9; I Cor. 13:8–13.

23. Bultmann, *History and Eschatology*, p. 152.

24. Luke 15:7, 10, 23, 32.

25. There is no evidence that Jesus himself understood his death as necessary in order to induce God to reconcile himself to the world, or to grant forgiveness to sinners. He did, evidently, expect that shortly after his death the Kingdom of God would come.

26. Ezek. 36:26, 28, 31; cf. 16:59–63.

Index

SUBJECTS

Names

Scripture References